To Joan and ... [illegible]
We could keep ... [illegible]
Your visit was a pleasure ... [illegible]
hope you return to Mayville
Jayne Blodgett Murray
or Noodles
8/19/14

M000092188

Jayne Blodgett Murray

The River's Bend

Memoirs of Mayville, Modeling, and JFK's Blue Jeans

The River's Bend
Memoirs of Mayville, Modeling, and JFK's Blue Jeans

Jayne B. Murray
As Told to and Edited by Judith Adamson
Jayne Gohr, Photo Editor

Copyright 2010
All Rights Reserved

No part of this book may be reproduced or transmitted in any form or by any means, electronic or mechanical, including photocopying, recording, or by any information storage and retrieval system, without the written consent of the publisher

ISBN 1-884820-549
978-1-884820-540
Library of Congress Catalog Card Number 2010923606
Categories: 1. Autobiography, Personal Memoirs
2. Murray, Jayne B.
3. Mayville, WI   4. History, Social

Printed in the United States of America
Safe Goods is committed to saving the environment through printing this book on recycled paper that contains a minimum of 30% post-consumer waste. At Safe Goods it's our goal to reduce our carbon footprint and at the same time further education about environmental issues.

Published by ATN/Safe Goods
561 Shunpike Rd., Sheffield MA 01257
413-229-7935
www.safegoodspub.com

To My Mother

CONTENTS

Part I: Mayville, Early Years-1947

Part II: New York, 1947-1951

Part III: Bedford, 1951-1993

Part IV: Narrowsburg, 1993-1998

Part V: Mayville, 2000-

Part 1

෨
Mayville: The Early Years-1947

My grandfather and my brother Billy on the bank of the Rock River across from Grandpa's house. Timed photo by CW, circa 1928.

Introduction

Mayville, Wisconsin hugs both banks of the Rock River. Main Street, where my school was, follows the river's contours on one side, and my childhood home sat on the other side. Every school day I crossed the river by footbridge four times—to school in the morning, home for lunch, back to school and home again. I assumed every child lived in a town with a river and a small bridge which they crossed every day as I did. It wasn't until I moved away that I realized not every town had a river and a footbridge like Mayville's.

I loved going over that bridge, listening to my shoes on the wooden planks and the different sounds the water made underneath—rushing and loud in spring, gurgling late summer into fall, or dead silent when ice overtook it in winter. I often dawdled in the middle to look over the rail to see what leaf boat might be headed for a fall over the dam. Sometimes I went under the bridge—although warned by my mother not to—to look for frogs and special rocks.

If it weren't for the river, there wouldn't be a Mayville. The Rock River, a distant tributary of the Mississippi, rises in the Theresa Marsh about seventeen miles south of Fond du Lac, winds southwest through lush meadows and groves, through Mayville, into the Horicon Marsh, south out of the marsh to pick up the Crawfish, the Bark and the Yahara Rivers, meanders into Illinois to receive the Pecatonica River, and edges westward before it finally joins the Mississippi at Rock Island.

The river and surrounding area must have been strikingly beautiful in their pristine state when the Fox, Potawatomi and Ho-Chunk lived here. My imagination, fired up by all the books I read, conjured up images as I stood on the footbridge—braves navigating the river in their canoes as they fished for plentiful bullhead, children jumping from the banks to swim in the pure water, and light reflecting off the river from evening campfires.

Inevitably, explorers and entrepreneurs discovered the area. In 1845, two sets of English brothers, the Fosters and the Mays, realizing the great potential of the region for farmland and industry, chose a bend in the river where they founded Mayville. They erected two dams to widen the river, enabling them to harness its power for running a sawmill, a grain mill and Wisconsin's first iron smelter.

German immigrants, drawn by the area's uncanny resemblance to their homeland, eagerly settled in Mayville. Soon dairy farms dotted the countryside, a schoolhouse and firehouse were built, a carriage and wagon factory established, a barbershop opened, and even a cigar factory was founded. Mayville grew by leaps and bounds over the next several decades, and it was into this exciting young boomtown that my grandfather, Christian William Docter, rode in 1885.

Christian William Docter, timed self portrait in his studio. Circa 1890.

∞ 1 ∞

Mayville Roots

A t the age of seventeen, "with only a penny in his pocket" as he was proud of saying, my grandfather made the hundred-mile journey up to Mayville from Kenosha where his parents had emigrated from Germany in the 1840s. Having apprenticed to a photographer there, CW, as he was known, had acquired the skills to work for the only photographer here in Mayville, and within a few years had accumulated enough money to buy him out. When he was settled, he sent for his sweetheart, Anna Moeller, and they married in 1890. They had John, then my mother Adelaide, Rudolph, Helen and Viola.

Wedding Day, 1890. l-r: unknown, CW (seated), Herb Kohler, unknown,Anna (seated), Lotte Schroeder Kohler

*Pushing into Lake Michigan: l-r: Anna Moeller (my grandmother),
Lotte Schroeder Kohler, Frances Raft, John Orth, CW. Circa 1888.*

I wish I knew more about Grandpa's early years, but I
seem to remember hearing that he only went through 8th
grade, and that he had a stepfather who gave him good reason to run away from home. His real father had fought in the
Civil War, only to die by falling off the church steeple in Kenosha when he was repairing it. Grandpa's lack of formal
education certainly didn't deter him from being a man of vi-
sion and becoming a successful entrepreneur in several en-
terprises in Mayville. He cut a well-known figure on Main
Street, often walking down the street with hands clasped behind his back, probably contemplating his next business venture as he nodded 'hello' and stopped to chat.

Mayville, early 1900s. Photo by CW Docter.

My grandfather eventually moved his studio from Main Street to a building he constructed on Bridge Street. The C.W. Docter Photography Studio was a very successful

CW, younger years.

business, fitting neatly into a slot in time when people wanted documentation of memorable events, but the personal camera had not yet been invented. His only competition was a photographer way up in Fond du Lac, so from miles around people came to CW's studio for portraits, graduation photos, baby pictures, anniversary pictures and, of course, wedding photos. He must have photographed over 2,000 wedding portraits. Considered the City of Mayville's official photographer, CW, when he wasn't in his studio, was out shooting parades down Main Street, picnics in the park, and all the end-of-school-year class photographs.

Not content with just one business venture, CW saw great potential in magic lantern shows, which were kind of a precursor to motion pictures. These shows were all the rage—a combination of live drama and music accompanied by images from hand-colored slides projected on a full-sized screen by a machine called a lantern. CW took his two oldest children with him, traveling by horse and wagon all over the county, to perform these shows.

Original studio, 1890s.

John played the violin and my mother Addie, with her beautiful voice, sang as CW worked the slides—many with exotic special effects—changing them every thirty seconds.

Docter's Novelty Shop was his next venture, created mostly because he felt his children should have something productive to do after school. They all had to work there at some time or other, learning how to make change and run the business. There were magazines, gifts, and school supplies like pencils and tablets, along with ice cream with a choice of several different handmade sauces. Grandpa would bring home a crate of strawberries or pineapples, which the children had to clean so my grandmother could boil them down into a rich, delicious sauce. Ice cream cones were well worth it at five cents and sundaes at ten cents; with a topping, a few cents more.

Rudolph (l) and John Docter, circa 1900.

CW set John and Rudolph up with a fancy popcorn wagon in downtown Mayville. With the smell of freshly popped corn wafting down Main Street, it didn't take long for my uncles to gather a crowd and turn a little profit.

Besides being one of the foremost businessmen in Mayville, CW was community minded. He was an investor in *The Mayville News;* he became a member of the school board, wanting to have a say in how the children of Mayville were educated at the White Limestone School. He was very interested in Mayville's history and its government, although he never ran for office. Later in his life he became a great one for clipping things out of newspapers and writing letters to the editor of *The Mayville News*, usually letting Viola draft the letters because he was such a terrible speller.

Helen (l), Addie (center), Viola Docter, circa 1902.

CB

When my mother was a girl, the family lived right on the river on South Main Street. In the summer they could jump in for a swim from their front yard and in the winter

they could skate several miles up the frozen river to the next bridge. Grandpa had a boat named Modjeska after the famous Russian actress, and toyed with the idea of having a channel in the river cleared so he could offer boat trips all the

The Docters' house on South Main St.

way up to a neighboring town named Theresa. It would be a commercial venture where he took people on day trips, starting above the upper dam where he had a boathouse. It would have been a good way to connect the two towns, but the idea never made it past the conceptual stage.

The Modjeska at "Upper Dam" launch on the Rock River.
l-r, Helen, John and assorted guests. Circa 1910.

I got the feeling from my mother that the Docter family was close. There's a wonderful photo by CW that hangs on my study wall with the whole family posing, but not in the usual family portrait way. Instead, it tells a story, which would have been unusual for those times and would be considered more of an artistic shot. In the center is a large tree with Viola, the youngest in the family, sitting on a branch in

L-r: Rude, Angie, Helen, Addie, Viola, John, Anna. Photo by CW, circa 1904.

her pinafore. On the ground, my mother in her school clothes, Helen, John, Rudolph, their mother and Aunt Angie stand calmly, looking up at Viola. What's striking is the feeling of the captured moment and the curiosity the photo provokes as to what's going on. The technique is remarkable in its clarity of detail—the bark of the tree, the wood fence behind the tree, every leaf on the ground—all incredibly sharp. You feel like you're right there in the photograph.

All CW and Anna's children had been baptized Catholic since Grandpa was a Catholic. When my mother was seven she was frightened out of her wits and right out of the Catholic Church by a visiting priest preaching fire and brimstone and going to hell. My mother got so scared that she ran out of church, went home and hid under the bed. My grandfather, incensed, stormed up to the priest and told him that none of his children were going to a church where they'd be frightened. He never went to church after that and told my mother and her brothers and sisters that they could choose whatever church they wanted to attend. My mother's siblings picked the Methodist because it had music and get-togethers for youth.

As a young woman, my mother was very pretty. I know this by CW's photos of her. She was really quite thin but never looked that thin because she had a big bosom which, she told me later, she gladly would have had reduction surgery for if it had been an option in those days. In one of my grandfather's photos he captures her wistful look. Her hair is done up in the Gibson Girl 'do' of the times—all gathered, swept up and rolled around a horsetail "rat," giving it the fashionable width that went so well with her unbelievably tiny waist. There's something about the photograph—a softness and intimacy that tells me CW was very fond of her. Along with that fondness, however, came the fact that CW was very strict and protective of his daugh-

Mother, 1919.
Photo by CW.

A day in the country. l-r: John, CW with Viola, Rude, Angie, Helen, Anna, Addie, circa 1920. Timed photo by CW.

13

ters; he didn't want them to go to the dances up at the Park Pavilion because he thought it was beneath their station.

Grandpa took his last name very seriously; in fact, it was a sign, he thought, and vowed that his sons would become doctors. Although John wanted to play the violin and Rudolph wanted to be a minister, my grandfather insisted they become doctors because their last name was Docter! They didn't have a choice. My Uncle John became Dr. Docter, a pediatrician, and Uncle Rude became Dr. Docter, a dentist. At one point they were even in *Ripley's Believe It or Not* as the Doctor Docters!

Above: CW photographing my mother (timed photo); Left, Docter's Novelty Store

My mother, knowing that she wouldn't have the chance to go to college after high school, was determined to continue to educate herself. She made a practice of reading at least one article a day in a magazine.

While her brothers went off to college, she worked at Docter's Novelty Store after graduating high school. That's where she met my father.

William Morris Blodgett was a good eleven years older than she was, and had come to Mayville from Randolph to run the Mayville Canning Factory. He must have stopped in the store one hot day for an ice cream, and he and Addie began talking.

My father's father, Morris Riley Blodgett, had made his living in farming and lumber. He fought in the Civil War and died well before I was born; hearsay tells us that he was killed by a log falling on him at the lumber mill when he was around forty. Unfortunately, my grandmother on my father's side, Kate Isabelle Stark Blodgett, died a year after I was born, so I never really knew her. My father never talked about her, so all I know is what my mother said about her. She gave me the impression that she was not particularly fond of Kate who was a teacher, an artist, and wrote some very good poetry. The only story I remember is that when she died and they were taking her to be buried, there was a huge snowstorm; the hearse slipped off the road and overturned—coffin and all—in a ditch. I shudder to think of the ensuing scene.

In 1917, the same year my mother met her husband-to-be, CW added yet another business to his entrepreneurial repertoire. He bought the Modjeska Theater—the only movie theater for miles around. Later he changed its name to the May Theater. People couldn't get enough of the movies, and as had happened with his photography studio, CW had launched another business that boomed in the most advantageous time possible. He just seemed to have a knack. When the movie let out, everyone went over to the Docter's Novelty Store for ice cream.

The theater was a family run affair. Viola's husband, "Mert" Miller, ran the projector while my mother played the melodeon—the same one that sits in my hallway today. Moving pictures had no sound at that time, so to enhance the silent film, CW bought the melodeon and had it shipped all the way from Buffalo, New York to Mayville. It was beautifully handcrafted out of rosewood, with not quite a full keyboard, a pump, and two foot pedals. Since everyone took music lessons in those days, my mother could play it, but she had to pump it at the same time she was playing the keys so it was a little uneven. A few years later CW bought an organ with all sorts of elaborate sound effects. It sat down in the orchestra pit, and by pushing and pulling different buttons my mother could get sounds like a train whistle or horses galloping, which added immensely to the silent pictures. When the theater was remodeled in the 1930s, stairs were built right over the melodeon, hiding it for a number of years until they pulled out the stairs. At that point, my mother salvaged it and took it to our house. I shipped it to New York after I got married and in 2000 shipped it back to Mayville where it rests in my front hall, so it's been going back and forth between New York and Wisconsin for almost a hundred years.

ભ

According to my mother, CW had his quirks, or perhaps was just way ahead of his time. Although he owned a car, for some reason never learned to drive, so he had one of his sons, or later my brother, drive him around. He was a devotee of Bernarr MacFadden, a well-known health proponent at the time, and Grandpa himself was apparently a complete health nut. He believed people should get out and do "physical culture," as it was called in those days. Germans are very much for that anyway; they had a term for it—*turnverein*—and people in Mayville would meet en masse in a big hall called Turner's Hall to wield dumbbells together. There are pictures of Grandpa in one of those strapped black, wooly bathing suits that men wore, posing like Mr. Universe. He also had an exercise gizmo that fastened to the top of the door and a machine with a belt that went around the waist; when you turned it on it massaged you, jiggling off the calories, I suppose. He had a bathtub he sat in called a 'sitz' bath that he thought was good for his kidneys. It was more like a big washbasin with maybe a few minerals thrown in.

Grandpa got unprocessed, whole grain flour from a mill outside of town, which my grandmother baked into wholesome bread. He also made sure his children had apples all winter so he'd stock up on a couple of barrels. My mother told me how she and her brothers and sisters used to go to school with their apples every day, well beyond apple season, and all the other children stood around enviously watching as they ate them, begging for the apple core when they were done. Grandpa also used to make vegetable juice. In later years, he got a machine that mixed up carrots and other vegetables and made these awful concoctions which he drank all the time. He didn't believe in eating much meat, which I imagine was unusual in those times.

My mother told me how he'd get an idea and then proceed to overdo it. Once he decided that watermelon was good for him so he ate an entire watermelon and then wondered why he felt sick. Grandpa lived to seventy-eight, not a particularly ripe old age, but Uncle John died at a hundred-and-eight, my mother at ninety-seven and Aunt Viola at eighty-seven, so all that whole wheat bread and apples must have done something for his children.

My mother's younger sister Helen, whom she adored, was kind of a tomboy who liked to ride in the sidecar of her brother's motorcycle, row the boat up and down the Rock River and play tennis. She also took after her father and loved photography. She was engaged to a man named Warren who lived out in Washington state. In 1920 when Helen was only twenty-four, she boarded the train to Fond du Lac for a simple goiter operation. My mother told me how the family all waved goodbye to her at the train station, looking forward to her return in a couple of days, but she never made it back. She died during the operation—a terrible shock and devastating tragedy for my mother and the rest of the family.

I'm sure Helen's death hit my grandfather as hard as anybody. I get the idea that he was not very eager to see his two remaining daughters married, which may explain my parents' long engagement of five years, or perhaps in those days people had the sense to be engaged longer. Aunt Viola married late in life also and never had children.

Finally, my parents married in 1922, and went to a canning convention in Louisville for their honeymoon. They stayed at the elegant Seelbach Hotel, comparable to New York's famous Waldorf Astoria. I'm sure it was quite exciting for them.

Left: My great grandmother, Elizabeth, (1842-1920); married to my great grandfather, John Docter, (1842-1866). Below: Kate Stark Blodgett, my paternal grandmother (1852-1928).

L-r: Angie, Addie, Helen, Rude, Grandma Puls (CW's stepmother). Photo by CW, circa, 1900.

18

*Left, top to bottom: Addie, Great Aunt Margaret Moeller,
Frances Moeller Bauer; top right: Aunt Angie Moeller,
Tillie Moeller Ewing. Photo by CW. Early 1900s*

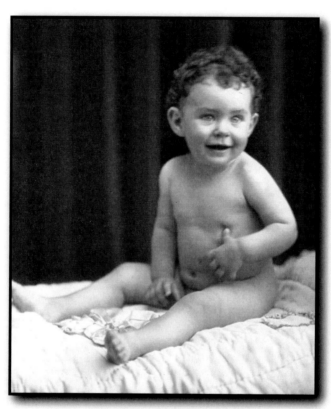

Me, 1927 taken by Grandpa in his studio.

∽ 2 ∾
The Blodgetts of North German Street

*M*other was close to thirty and my father forty-one by the time they had Billy. I was born three-and-a-half years later in 1926. We lived on North German Street, only a few doors down from where I live now.

As a young child, I was chubby and cute with long, ringlet finger curls that my mother made every day. Billy wore knickers and argyle socks. My mother always said she raised Billy to be too gentle, but in my eyes he was my sweet, big brother who was always protective of me. I called him Billy, but when we were little, everybody else called me "Sister" and him "Brother." That was until I was seven or eight.

Me at age two, taken by Grandpa in his studio.

Billy holding me on his lap on the steps of our childhood home on North German Street. 1927

On Grandpa's front steps. Back, l-r: Uncle John, Mother, Uncle Rude; center l-r: Grandma with me, Grandmother Puls with my cousin Grant, my cousin Jack Docter; front, l-r: my cousin Jean Docter, Billy, my cousin Bill Docter. Photo by Grandpa, 1927.

Daddy and me, 1931. Photo by Grandpa in his studio.

Mother and me, 1929. Photo by Grandpa in his studio.

When I was about five, Billy got scarlet fever and had to be quarantined. The officials put a big red sign on our door; no one was allowed to enter the house, and I had to go stay with Grandpa and Grandma for three weeks. My mother wasn't even allowed to come out and kiss me or hug me, so I'd go stand in our yard and look longingly at her through the window. I was really homesick with my mother and brother locked up in the house. Billy was in bed for many months after the scarlet fever to the point where he had to learn to walk all over again. He eventually recovered, but it left him weak and vulnerable to rheumatic fever, which I would also struggle with a few years later.

Neither of my parents went to church, but clearly they wanted to give us some exposure to organized religion. Mother had been scared off by the hell-mongering priest, and I don't remember ever seeing my father in church. When I was five years old my mother took me over to the Methodist Sunday School where the large sandbox raised on a table made a great impression on me. It seemed huge; you could stand at it and make sand castles, which I thought was great. Apparently that clinched my religious choice. Billy and I went to church regularly as long as we lived in Mayville. I sang in the junior choir and once I was Mary in the Christmas pageant. Even my being the mother of Christ couldn't get my mother to come to church.

After Sunday School, Father would often pick Billy and me up and drive us to Butch's Tavern in neighboring Kekoskee where his hunting buddy, "Butch" Burkhart, ran his establishment. My father stood casually at the bar—just like in the movies—and drank a shot of whiskey out of a little glass. Only he didn't toss it back in one gulp; instead he nursed one drink the entire hour we were there. Billy and I got a glass of soda and played the pinball machine. Then my father drove us back home for Sunday lunch, sometimes stopping to pick wildflowers in the woods. Father knew all about plants—peas and corn and Jack in the Pulpits—and where to find them because much of the time he was visiting farms for his job.

Sunday lunch was a big occasion. Mother would have made a roast chicken or roast beef and we ate in the dining

Christmas, 1932. Me, Mother, Billy, Daddy. Photo by Grandpa.

room using the good silver, whereas other days we ate in the kitchen seated at a round table. For dessert there was always ice cream, which cost 25 cents a quart, and was usually delivered by the owner of the drug store on his way home to his own Sunday dinner.

My father had a wonderfully dry sense of humor, but was naturally a very quiet man. In my memory, he was mostly in the background except when it came to decisions like whether Billy or I were going to be punished, which was seldom; then he became the central figure. I remember sitting on his lap but I can't remember ever hugging him; he was more of an authoritative figure. I must have been a fairly well-behaved little girl, because I only had three spankings when I was growing up, one from my mother and the other two from my father. I only remember the specifics of one. I was playing with my dolls in the library on a little wooden table one evening. Billy and I mostly got along very well, but for some reason he was pestering me for the table before I was ready to give it up, and finally I said to him, "Take your shit piss table." My father put down his newspaper and said, vehemently for him, "What did you say?" I repeated it, and he spanked me, not a big deal over his knees with a paddle or anything, but enough of a wop on my behind that it made quite an impression. I ran upstairs to my mother, telling her that Daddy had just spanked me. My mother only said, "Well you know...." She didn't take my side, which was probably a very healthy reaction.

On Saturday mornings Billy and I often went to Grandpa's studio. He had toys for children to keep them busy while he photographed their parents, and we liked to go and play with them. He often took pictures of us as we played.

Mother always wanted us dressed up and looking proper; I had a bow in my hair no matter what, and she made perfect finger curls every day. Billy often wore one of those leather flying caps, goggles and lace-up boots which had been made popular in the late 1920s because hero Charles Lindbergh

Me at Grandpa's studio, circa 1931.

25

wore them. One of Grandpa's photos shows the two of us, Billy in his Lindbergh outfit and me wearing a fur coat my mother made out of the fur lining of a coat, which Mr. Means, who ran the iron company, had given her awhile back.

One day my fur coat got soaking wet from wearing it in a snowstorm. I was down at my grandmother's house and she put it on the radiator to dry. She called up that night and said the coat had cracked into pieces and had totally fallen apart because the leather had dried out!

cx

Billy and me at Grandpa's studio, circa 1932.

My childhood spanned much of the Depression. I remember it in a way, but it seems in retrospect as if people were much closer in those days, always ready to help each other out; I don't remember it being a hard time. Maybe we were protected since my father's job was in management, so never in question. Also, canning factories were very important in those days. People had to eat, so the factories were able to make ends meet, even during the Depression. I never felt deprived.

In 1933, on the day the banks closed, I came home from school for lunch and I could sense that my parents were upset about something. Of course I didn't understand what was going on, but my mother said that when I went back to school be sure to tell Mrs. Bennett that the banks had closed. She wanted me to go back to school and sound really smart, I think. I can still remember my sense of importance as I made this announcement to my teacher. I didn't know what it meant, but it seemed very serious.

Photo of me by Grandpa in his studio, circa 1931.

Me at the age of ten, 1936. Photo by Grandpa in his studio.

❧ 3 ❧

My Life in Books

$\mathcal{M}$uch of my childhood was spent in bed, and I lived in books. When I was nine I got rheumatic fever, which probably developed after I had strep throat. Some people just have a genetic weakness for it, which clearly Billy and I both did. Once you had it, it recurred sporadically. It could be triggered by a mere cold, so every time I even sneezed or had a sore throat I had to be extra careful. Rheumatic fever, which people rarely get anymore, was quite common back when I was a child and could be life threatening. It often affected the heart muscle, which is why I had to be very careful and not exert myself throughout my whole childhood and young adulthood.

I wasn't allowed to run and never learned to ride a bicycle. I had just started to learn to roller skate and ice skate, but after I developed rheumatic fever I was never allowed to skate again. I wasn't supposed to walk up and down many steps, including the steps at school. My mother enlisted the services a couple of girls in my class to tell her if I ran during recess.

When I was really sick I was taken out for a "walk" to get me out in the fresh air. This meant being rolled around in a cart that had been hand made by our next door neighbor, Mr. Hollenstein, who had the carriage and wagon shop that's now the Historical Society. The Hollensteins were a Swiss family that came to Mayville in the 1870s. Since Billy and I couldn't pronounce Hollenstein we used to call them Aunt Hattie and Uncle John. I hated going out in that cart because people always stopped to talk, and I thought they felt sorry for me. I really wasn't incapacitated; I could have walked and run if my mother had let me. Sometimes I feel she was over-protective, but considering how healthy Bill and I are now, she probably did the right thing, especially around nutrition.

My mother listened to my grandfather and fed us health foods like wheat germ, raisins, prunes, whatever fruits and vegetables she could get. In winter there were only about six different vegetables available. She made sure we had hot cereal in the winter, and every morning gave us cod liver oil, to which she added lemon juice to cut the fishy taste, making it more palatable. She did the same with a thick molasses-like vitamin.

I remember going with my mother to the store. Everything was behind the counter and you had to ask the grocer to take what you wanted off the shelf. The first supermarket I ever went to was just before the war. It was a Piggly Wiggly in Fond du Lac and we made a special trip there. It was the first time we ever went through a grocery store with a cart and picked out our own food.

Uncle John, who lived in Racine, was one of the first pediatricians around, and my mother constantly consulted him on Billy's and my condition. Sometimes she thought he was being overly cautious, but to err on the safe side, she took everything he said literally. She called him regularly and he came up to Mayville often to look in on us. Of course we had a local doctor, but my mother really depended on her brother.

Billy was sick with rheumatic fever so much that sometimes we overlapped when we were both bedridden. Between the two of us, we kept my mother hopping. Billy was in one room and I was in the other, so we had to talk across the hall. My mother had two trays of meals that she brought up three times a day. Our temperatures had to be taken very regularly, and it seemed every time she got near us she took our pulse—probably at least eight times a day. She kept meticulous records on long strips of paper on the wall. There were so many she could have papered the whole house with them.

Not only did my mother minister to our physical infirmities, she also provided us with books and projects to keep us engaged instead of bored. I remember her being cheerful, and I don't imagine all mothers with two sick, bedridden children would have handled it as gracefully as she did.

Sometimes during the day we'd be allowed in the same bedroom. Then we'd put on plays with Valentines, using the sheets as a stage. We looked at lots of old *National Geographics* and made up stories from the pictures. Ads for Chris Craft boats were a gold mine—we each picked out a boat and pretended we were taking trips, telling elaborate stories of our navigations. Billy loved airplanes and wanted to be pilot, so he built model airplanes and regaled me with stories about where he was flying. We made up endless games.

We each missed a whole year of school and both ended up a grade behind. I was absent a lot between 3rd and 5th grades; somebody had to bring me my homework every day or two and my mother helped me with whatever I needed to study. I remember I was in the class where you just started to learn handwriting, so it fell to her to teach me.

There was so much I couldn't do, but on the other hand, the much larger world of books and imagination was totally open to me. I didn't mind staying in bed, and when I look back on it, I realize I didn't really want to go back to school. I could read all the time and listen to soap operas on the radio. I remember it as being a very happy time and feeling very secure. Often my mother read aloud to me, and Grandma and Aunt Angie often came and read. When Billy and I were sick together, the choice of books had to interest us both so I was brought up fast to his level. Cowboys, Indians, pioneers, adventurers, dogs—there didn't seem to be anything I wasn't interested in.

My mother went to the library and brought back maybe eight books at a time. I'd have read four or five of them already because she couldn't keep track of all the books I was reading. I loved to read about Indians and knew the names of every tribe in the country. I was fascinated by stories of the early days of the settlers. I read the complete series of *The Bobsey Twins* and *Nancy Drew*, *The Wind in the Willows* and *Black Beauty*. I loved Albert Payson Terhune who wrote about collies. I adored the *Honey Bunch* series which was geared toward ten to twelve-year-olds where the little girl goes on all these first trips—first visit to the city, first days on a farm, first trip to the seashore, etc. My favorite was *Honey Bunch: Her First Trip West*. She felt like a contemporary because her family had an automobile like the one we had.

I used to draw pictures and make up stories in my head—mostly about knights, ladies and horses—to go with my drawings. I loved it when my mother told stories of her childhood or recited the historical epic poems of Longfellow.

For a treat and to change the scene, Mother sometimes put bedding on the sofa in the living room and I went down there for the late afternoon and early evening. I was lying on the sofa the day Grandpa came in, crying, and told my mother that my grandmother had died. It was during an operation, possibly for goiter, but she got pneumonia, which is what she actually died of. That image of Grandpa crying is still vivid, and I still remember how sad it made me.

My great aunt Angie stepped in and became our "grandmother" after that. Angela had come from Kenosha when she was about fifteen to help her sister Anna when she was having her first baby, and she never went home. For some reason she never married and always lived in my grandparents' house. Photos of her as a young woman show how beautiful she was with big eyes and dark hair. When Billy and I were sick she'd walk from the other side of town to come read to us, often bringing us ice cream cones.

In 1936 when I was ten, we went to Biloxi, Mississippi for the winter to stay away from the cold in an attempt to ward off another attack of rheumatic fever. My father drove us down, left the car with us, and returned to Mayville by train. He came back to pick us up in the spring.

Mississippi in the middle of the Depression was right out of *The Grapes of Wrath;* people in overalls rode in ox-carts and were out picking cotton in the fields. We had a very pleasant time down there, however. We rented a house and went to the library every couple of days, then sat out by the water, reading Dr. Doolittle books. I still have some photos of our time in Biloxi. One shows some people walking along a dusty road. There's one of me in the branches of an olive tree reading a book. I used to think it was romantic to climb a tree and perch on a branch to read. There's a photo of a dog we had when we were there. I'm not sure if he might have

Billy, me and our "borrowed" dog. Biloxi, 1936

been a stray or belonged to the woman whose house we rented. I hope he wasn't a stray because we had to leave him there.

Mother and me in Biloxi. 1936

❧

If, perhaps, I was a little out of step with other children my age it wasn't that I was behind in school. It was because I read so much that my world was vast and my knowledge way beyond most children my age. My childhood, lived so much in the company of books, was a gift, and I consider each book I read a dear old friend.

Mother, Gypsy and me in Grandpa's back yard,
circa 1941.

CR 4 SO

The Awkward, Gawky Years

I must have gotten my entrepreneurial spirit from Grandpa. Between ten and twelve years old I had a thriving business during the summer selling drinks at the Mayville Canning Company, which didn't have dispensers for cold drinks. The fact that my father ran the canning factory was the only reason I was allowed to do this.

My mother drove me and a friend, another little girl who had rheumatic fever and whose mother worked during the day, to the Mayville Bottling Company to buy a whole case of soda for 65 cents—24 bottles of assorted flavors, which came in glass bottles in a wooden box. I borrowed the initial "capital" from my parents and paid it back as soon as I had made the 65 cents. We had the soda all iced, and my mother dropped my "helper" and me at the canning factory where we put the drinks in a wagon. We added frozen Milky Ways, which we bought three for a dime and sold for 5 cents apiece. We pulled the wagon through the canning factory and sold cold drinks and frozen candy bars in the afternoon to the men. I paid my help each day with a soda and a candy bar. At the end of the summer I had a grand total of $12 or $13 profit and, knowing me, I probably put it all in the bank.

Main Street, Mayville. 1940s.

೦೩

I had another attack of rheumatic fever when I was twelve, which left me with a heart murmur. We went to a specialist in Milwaukee where I had an electrocardiogram, a very new kind of procedure then. The doctor told my mother I might only live to be twenty-nine years old which must have absolutely terrified her. You'd think he would have at least rounded it off to thirty!

Grandpa took a photo of me with my mother around this age. It shows me as kind of an awkward, gawky teenager. I was very tall and scrawny, wore glasses and had braces on my teeth. My mother always made sure I looked the best I could, brushed my hair every day until I was ten, and often had a local dressmaker make a special suit or dress for me. I didn't think I was the least bit pretty. Half the time I walked around without glasses thinking I looked better; con-sequently, I couldn't see anything or anybody at school. Bill had bad eyes too; we were both very near sighted. My mother's theory was we read so much in bed without proper lighting that that was why we had bad eyesight, but I think it was hereditary in the Blodgett family.

Mother was somewhat strict, but also very loving. Sometimes I think she was more like an older sister, which often isn't good, but to my thinking she never overplayed it. She was a very kind person, not only to me but also to people she didn't know very well. She'd do things like bake a birthday cake for the little boy down the street because his family didn't have much money and they had four or five children. Mother didn't work in any job; it just wasn't done in those days. I remember she dressed up every day no matter what; it simply wouldn't have occurred to her to go to the market without dressing up—hat and all. She just loved hats and especially loved to pose in them for a photo. People remember her as being very regal.

Pen and ink rendering of the White Limestone School I drew for our yearbook, The Rocket.

I had talent for drawing and painting, which perhaps I inherited from my grandmother Kate, who was an artist as well as a schoolteacher. When I was quite young, I copied a small newspaper picture of a painting I liked using pastels. Mother wanted to nurture my artistic ability and sent me to private art lessons from the school art teacher, who worked with me and another girl. When I was twelve, I won a runner-up prize for the Wisconsin Dairy Products Poster Contest given by the Mayville Junior Women's Club. I had to draw a picture on a big poster to go with the slogan "Wisconsin Cheese is Sure to Please." I don't remember what I drew, but I got a letter from Phillip La Follette congratulating me for a fine entry. The La Follettes were a very famous political family and Robert La Follette was a nationally known senator. I won $2.50 and Grandpa gave me another $5.00 because he was so proud of me. Another poster contest that I entered had to do with saving wildlife, and I won First Prize—$5.00. I still have that poster. It's large and shows a deer caught in the snow, his front legs out straight, as a forest ranger kneels down near him.

I always loved animals. We really didn't have stray animals around when I was growing up, and I didn't know about animal shelters; in fact, I'm not sure they had them then. I always wanted a pony, and Billy always wanted a hippopotamus. Neither of us understood why we couldn't have them. It seemed simple that a pony could just live in the back yard and Billy suggested the hippo could live in the cistern, a big scary stone partition in the basement where water was stored. I remember how excited I was when I got my first dog when I was about twelve years old. Her name was Gypsy and she was a little toy terrier. One time she needed an operation and Dr. Parish kindly operated on her, but told us not to tell anyone. Later, when I went away to school of course I couldn't take her and left her with my mother. In my letters, I always asked how Gypsy was and asked my mother to take good care of her (which she did), so she'd still be there when I came home in the summer. I think my mother actually got quite fond of Gypsy.

Most children in Mayville went to the White Limestone School from Kindergarten through 6th grade. From there we went to the Red Brick School next door until we finished high school. There was also a Catholic school and a few outlying small country schools that eventually fed into the

Red Brick School for high school. I remember every teacher I had who, most likely, were the same teachers Billy had. Our teachers, longtime members of the community, were considered almost like your minister; they were that revered and respected. My mother always liked to invite our teachers around for tea and I was just so thrilled. Most parents didn't do that, but my mother wanted to know them. I was always proud to have them come to our home, which my mother had made really lovely.

Mother and me in our living room. Photo by Grandpa. This is actually a photo I color-tinted, although here it appears in black and white.

When we first moved into the house on North German Street, the staircase rose from one end of the living room. In the '30s, Mother decided she wanted to put a fireplace where the stairs were, and actually move the stairs. The carpenter said it couldn't be done, but she figured a way to cut through a closet and make it work. She was very good at figuring all those things out.

I must have inherited the interior design gene from my mother. She decorated the house tastefully, but it wasn't at all fussy, just very comfortable. There was a lightness, which I think settled deeply into my psyche and influenced me later in my own design projects. Big windows with beautiful leaded glass across the top looked out to the street. Inside were lovely French doors that opened into a big living room where the melodeon sat in a prominent corner, and against the wall we had a beautiful, pale mohair sofa, kind of a soft, moss green. Mother was one of the first people to start using light colors on furniture instead of the dark, heavy fabrics most people still had. Another set of French doors led into the library, which only had one small set of bookshelves, but we called it the library anyway. There was always a vase of fresh lilacs or peonies—whatever was growing in our garden—that my mother placed on the melodeon. Today, I keep the same vase in the exact same spot on the melodeon, filled with gladiolas.

⌳

I think I got my love of politics from Grandpa. I remember stopping in at his house on Sundays when he, Uncle John, and Uncle Rudolph got together for lunch. I was probably about fifteen. They'd all be sitting around the dining room table, listening to one of the radio commentators of the day—Father Coughlin, Walter Winchell or Drew Pearson. Then they'd break into heated political discussions.

Grandpa gave me the chance to try out my ideas with him and learn to discuss political issues. He was very much against our getting into World War II, so this would have been before 1941. He was a

Grandpa in his later years.

committed isolationist, very anti-Russian, and against getting into the war on Britain's side. In retrospect, I think my grandfather was foresighted in realizing that Russia was not a real friend of the United States. I was for getting into the war alongside Britain, so we would sit and talk about it on the porch swing.

Mayville had a majority of German people with many who had relatives fighting in the war on the German side. Probably the sympathy for Germans was much more heated in World War I than in World War II. More years had elapsed, so being of German descent no longer had that weighted value that it had back in World War I.

Senior year high school picture.

๙ 5 ๛

The Glass Booth

My father died when I was fifteen although he had been ill for about five years before that. He had high blood pressure and back then doctors didn't know how to do anything for it. He had a stroke and recovered somewhat, but kept having strokes during the time I was in middle school. Since he had been incapacitated for so long, it wasn't really a shock when he died.

There's something I didn't know about my father until after his death, which might explain his reserve and emotional distance. My mother had taken some papers out of her safe deposit box and left them on the car seat when she went into a store to do an errand. I was with her and snuck a peek at them. I saw that he had been married before to a woman named Elizabeth and had had two daughters. His wife and daughters all died at once, probably from the flu pandemic around 1917. Mother had never told Billy or me anything about my father and he himself had never talked about it. All I knew was that he had lived in Randolph and came to Mayville to manage the Mayville Canning Company. My grandparents are buried in Randolph and we used to go over there on Memorial Day to visit the cemetery when I was small.

I remember my father being this quiet man, but gifted with a great sense of humor that Bill has too. He could be totally straight faced, and all of a sudden come out with a very funny remark. I never heard him get cross or swear. He always dressed for work very properly in a shirt and tie and was soft spoken and polite.

Top row, l-r: CW, Uncle Rude, my cousin Grant, Uncle John, Bill, Me; second row: my cousins Bill, Jack and Joanne. CW's back yard, circa 1944 or 1945.

After my father died, I sold tickets at Grandpa's movie theater every night. My mother thought it was good for me to have a job and I'm very glad I did it because it gave me something to do at night. I was a good student so I didn't have much studying to do, plus I wasn't very socially inclined.

I got a huge sum of $28 a month for working every night for two or three hours. I had to be there at 6:30 and the show started at 7:00. The theater seated two hundred people, and usually I'd sell every single ticket within that half hour. The price of the tickets was 33 cents for adults, 12 cents for children. The box office was a glass enclosure built right out onto the street and sometimes there was such a huge crowd that I worried they'd push and the glass would break.

When I first started the job I was so nervous I cried because I thought I wasn't pretty enough to sit out there on view since I wore glasses. I had to be dressed up every night to sell tickets. My mother loved to buy nice clothes for me, or sometimes she had things made by a dressmaker in town who could add touches like a fur collar or special buttons. She was always very careful about not letting me think I was pretty, not that she went out of her way to make me seem otherwise; she just didn't want me to focus on that.

Besides selling tickets, I also used to tint pictures at my grandfather's studio when I was in high school in order to make some extra money. Grandpa paid me a certain amount for each picture. I had little tubes of oil paint that smelled like an artist's studio, and I'd put the color on with cotton balls.

 C3

It was at the glass booth of the theater that I first saw Eric. I was aware of Eric Johnson because he had had a horrific automobile accident, and in Mayville everyone in town knew if something terrible like that happened. He nearly died, but Dr. Parish saved his life by getting to the accident scene immediately and telling people not to move him because his back was injured. Eric was partially paralyzed for almost a year. When he got better he used to come to the movie theater, always smiled and said hello to me in the glass booth. I was probably sixteen, and he was a good ten years older. He was tall and I thought very good-looking. My mother often took the tickets inside, and as she was taking his ticket he'd always visit with her, which most people did. The theater was the kind of a place where everyone stopped to chat for a few moments before taking a seat.

Sometimes Eric came up to the house, and my mother would fix him a drink. We never drank at home, but I guess she had a couple of bottles of liquor around for possible guests. One time I remember she had two half-empty bottles, and poured the bourbon in with the wine to consolidate. I hope that's not what she gave Eric, but if so, he was very gracious. I never knew for sure whether he liked me or just liked to come visit my mother. I honestly didn't know.

Eric's parents, along with an uncle, had come from Sweden, and they owned Mayville Die and Tool Company. It was not a small operation and employed quite a few men engaged in war work.

Eric had two golden retrievers and sometimes invited me over to see the dogs or take them for a walk. He knew I could draw and he asked me to do a portrait of his beautiful retriever, Czar of Wildwood, Czar for short. Not many people in Mayville had a dog of that quality. I did a large pastel painting using photographs to draw from and he came to my house often to look at the progress of the portrait. Finally I presented it to him and he was thrilled. Later he got me a commission from a man down in St. Louis who had the national field trial champion of black Labradors, so I painted a portrait of his dog.

Gypsy and me, striking a pose. Circa 1942.

Czar became the bench show champion. Eric started a field trial club for retrievers in Mayville, and he asked if I'd help make posters and put them up around town. By then I had developed a very strong crush on him and was always happy to help him.

Sometimes Eric asked me to go down to Milwaukee with him to do this or that. I was just thrilled, especially when we went to the dog trainer's where he had Czar for a while. Eric had a great sense of humor and was really a very interesting man. I loved to hear him talk, especially about dogs, and I'm sure that's where my love of dogs came from. When we returned from Milwaukee his parents, who were lovely people, sometimes asked me for dinner. I always felt like Eric's little sister, never like a date. I guess I'd call it a brother/sister relationship. The only trouble was I seemed to be falling in love with him. If he smoked a cigarette, I saved the matchbox he had touched to light his cigarette.

Doctor Parish, the doctor who had taken care of Eric after his accident, was also my doctor. He and his wife, who didn't have any children of their own, were good friends of the Johnsons and my family, so he knew much of what was going on, including that I liked Eric a lot. I went to their home often, hoping Eric might be visiting.

I found nothing appealing about the boys my age in high school. I couldn't imagine going out with a boy named Touchie, Boobie or Munga—nicknames they were actually proud of, which shows the level they were on. They were immature, and I especially disliked going to school dances where the boys just fooled around with each other leaving girls to be-bop with other girls. That was definitely not my idea of a good time.

Art Director of The Mayville Rocket.

I had a small cadre of girlfriends. In those days, we would have been considered the "brains" or "nerds," certainly not part of the popular or athletic group. I couldn't play any sports in school because of the rheumatic fever. I did a little archery, but that was all. By contrast, Billy was very popular; he was the prom king in high school and played the drums in the school dance band.

I was so shy that I'd cross the street in town in order not to talk to somebody on the other side of the street. I was always really scared to death to get up and talk in front of the class; I'd shake and lose my voice. Later when I went to college, I faced my fear and took a speech class. I just hated the class but went anyway, and although I started out with a C, by the end of the class I had an A.

Despite being in love with Eric, in my senior year I dated Fred Karston off and on. I met Fred, the son of the doctor in the next town, while I was selling tickets. He was very good-looking, had been in the Coast Guard and was in college. Eric would often joke around with me saying things like, "Oh I saw that Fred was over last night...." It seemed like he was being kind of a big brother.

I was a bit of a loner in high school but preferred it that way. I think I had been exposed to so much in books that I had a larger view of the world than other people my age. Besides, I worked in the evenings and would rather be reading in my free time. I also preferred to spend time with my mother's friends. Many afternoons we'd go to Auntie Bernice's or a friend of Mother's for tea. I loved listening to them talk and felt very comfortable joining in the conversations.

My pencil drawing (12 x18) of Czar, from a Kodak photo.

Highschool graduation photo, 1945.

≪ 6 ≫

Three Chances

First Chance

Mrs. Johnson invited my mother and me over for tea occasionally. There were the four of us sipping tea— me, Eric and our two chaperones, but it really wasn't necessary because Eric had never made any advances toward me. That was until one weekend right after I had graduated from high school when Mrs. Johnson invited Mother and me up to their cottage at Green Lake, which is about forty miles from here. It was one of the nicest places around where people, many from Chicago, had summer cottages. Mother had to go back to Mayville after the weekend, and Mrs. Johnson invited me to stay a couple days more, so there I was unchaparoned by my mother.

One evening Eric and I went to some friends' house for drinks, and we stayed late into the evening, talking and having a great time. When we came back we parked in the driveway, and that's when Eric kissed me. *Finally.* I had hardly ever kissed anybody at that point except Thor Thorgesson and Fred Karston a few times.

"The Kiss" occurred about midnight on July 16, 1945. I'll always remember that date because it was the day the first atomic bomb was tested (although, of course, I didn't

know it at that time; I found out a couple of years later). The incredible powers of the bomb that were unleashed changed the world forever but, unfortunately, I missed my first chance to allow The Kiss to change my life. When it came to "doing anything," which in our day we demurely called "necking," I was quite reserved and naive. I always wished I had been a little more sophisticated and knew more about what was going on, but I had been taught to be prudish. So, in that moment, I did nothing to encourage him, and I missed my first chance.

Eric before 1945. I stole this photo out of a scrapbook when having tea with Eric's mother at Green Lake.

I still have the diary I wrote in religiously for five years! The entry for that day was:

Today was wonderful, the best day of my life. We wore our swimming suits all day. Eric didn't swim but laid in the sun with me. He'd stick his foot in my face or stretch his arm over me. Rode in the Cris-craft a lot. Called me "his proud beauty" and told me to stretch out my "lovely chassis." Party at Olson's—had 3 highballs. Then we took Jack and Allan home and went out with Wilsons to a road house, had 2 Tom Collins. A lieutenant sat next to me when Eric went to the bathroom and another fellow said he'd take Eric fishing if I went. Wanted to know if we were brother and sister. Eric put his arm around me. He kissed me when we got home, said he wasn't going to tonight—that he'd been thinking of it for some time. It was wonderful. I love him so.

Kissing him is so wonderful. I felt just ok and can't explain it but out of this world!
        The next day:

...We left Green Lake about 10:00. Eric smiled so nicely when he came to breakfast—whistled "I Love You." He sat in the back, however. I visited with Mrs. Johnson...I was so homesick for the lake. Wish I could live it over again.

Eric came down from Green Lake occasionally that summer so I'd see him at the theater. I was always wondering what he was going to do next. At one point he referred to himself as my Uncle Eric, which wasn't a good sign.

After the war, the Johnsons sold Mayville Die and Tool. A newspaper article I've kept for sixty-five years said, "Mayville's most flourishing industry, changed ownership July 2." I wrote a note under it saying, "very bad news to me." That was because the Johnsons were going to move to California.

CB

I didn't start college in the fall; instead, I went out to visit Bill for about five weeks where he was stationed in Connecticut. I really wasn't eager to go off to college right then, partly because I was in love with Eric and was hoping for something to transpire between us.

Bill had stayed in Mayville for a while after graduating from from high school, and then he went to California and worked at Lockheed Aircraft until the fall. He was in the service but my mother, unbeknownst to him, was doggedly contacting the draft board, trying to get him out because he had had rheumatic fever, had had a mastoid and was very near sighted. Bill wanted to go to war, not be 4-F. Feelings ran high back in those days of World War II when young men were eager to go to war to protect their country. First he was in the anti-aircraft artillery around Washington, DC when they actually had anti-aircraft guns set up, but Mother got him changed to the Medical Core.

He was stationed in Farmington, Connecticut at Avon Old Farms, a recovery center for blind veterans. It looked like an old English country castle and had formerly been a boarding school for very rich boys, but the Army took it over to use as a hospital.

It was during the fall, and my first long trip out of Mayville. I took the train from Chicago to New York and then the train up to Connecticut. It was very exciting for me because I

Bill, 1944.

had never been east before and I really fell in love with the area. I was going back to my father's side of my family roots where Blodgetts had come over from England in 1637 and eventually settled in the Apple Valley area of Connecticut. My grandfather, Riley Morris Blodgett, came from Tunbridge, Vermont and fought in the Civil War. My great great grandfather, Nathan Blodgett, fought in the Revolutionary War. My grandmother, Kate Isabelle Stark, was from Old Lyme, Connecticut. I loved Connecticut, the rolling hills and the old trees, and kept a diary about how wonderful I thought the East was—so romantic and just like a storybook movie. I stayed at the Farmington Country Club, a charming old rambling building.

Bill was engaged to Margaret, whom he had met when she was a senior in high school. Avon had occasional tea parties, and the high school girls would come out and dance with the blinded veterans. Margaret came from a very close-knit family. She had one sister and three very good-looking brothers, one of whom, Ray, I dated briefly. He flew B-59s and was dashingly handsome in his bomber uniform. Bill, Margaret, Ray, and I sometimes went out dancing together. Her family loved getting together, especially when it involved music since they all sang very well and were quite musical.

That summer, Margaret came to Mayville with her best girlfriend, Jan, to meet my mother. Later that summer, Mother and I, Auntie Bernice, and Dr. Parish's wife Ruth all drove to Middletown, Connecticut for Bill and Margaret's wedding, in which I was a bridesmaid.

Bill and Margaret didn't have any children for about eight or nine years after they married. Then they had Mindy and exactly a year later, to the day, Bill. In his first semester at the University of Connecticut, Bill, who never smoked or drank and ate apples every day, discovered a very painful lump in his neck. Bill and Margaret took him down to the National Institute of Health where he was given chemotherapy that made him very susceptible to infection. He was sick less than six months and died of chicken pox because his immune system was so compromised. We didn't know how ill he really was, so his death was a shock.

Cʘ

After visiting Bill, I returned to Mayville and started college at the University of Wisconsin in Madison the following January, 1946. I was an art major, lived in one of the private rooming houses named Ann Emory Hall on Langdon Street, and became a member of Chi Omega sorority.

Eric and I had kept in touch by letter. I always scoured his letters for covert signs of love and was always thrilled if he signed one "Love, Eric" which wasn't every time. The following chatty letter shows his great sense of humor, but I remember being disappointed that he didn't sign it "Love".

22255 Mulholland Drive
Woodland Hills, California
February 18,1946

Dear Jayne,

        Hope everything is progressing well for you
at Madison. Wonder if you pledged a sorority ? Why not
relax some fine evening and sit down and write to me
about how you like the outside world.

        I should never have left you - here I have only
been gone a few monthes and already you have slipped
down the ladder to a point where you are carrying on
with Black Labrador men. Ye Gads, woman, what are you
thinking of ? By this time you have no doubt heard of
CZAR'S latest triumph - he really showed the San Francisco
crowd - how a Golden can get out and step in fast company.
The set of Rogers 1847 Silverware that he won is
an outstanding one - though being a bachelor I wish the
award had been a Cup or Trophy so that I could have more
use for it.

        This is an interesting place - everyone you
meet either raises dogs or horses; acts, writes or does
something for the movies; is making a mint by some
hook or crook; or if they have nothing on the ball try to
be sophisticated and boast of their broad outlook on
morals and life in general. Have met some very fine
people but they are strictly in the minority - most of
those out here are so busy trying to impress others that
they never have time to develop themselves. You should
come out here some time and see some of these fine
specimans of the human race. Aye tank aye go back to
Visconsin !

        Now for the Kennel News ! FLASH ! It is
rumored that BEAUTYWOOD INSPIRATION (that outstanding
b _-- h whom has been seen so often in the company of
that prominent man about the fireposts, CZAR OF WILDWOOD,
is expecting a blessed event ! We can not divulge (never
could spell it) state at this time who the proud father
is - though we do have our suspicions ! This event should
take place about the first of March - will keep you
informed as to the ultimate outcome !

        As you can see by this letter, we are now
in our new place and it looks as if we all should enjoy
it. Moving delayed my answering your letter before - but
I won't be able to use this excuse again - so drop me
a line and be amazed at the quick response. Best regards
to your room-mate, she can't be as horrible as you picture
her. There, that should help you along if she is in the
habit of reading your mail.

                        Sincerely,
                            Eric

Second Chance

I was pleasantly surprised when twenty red roses from Eric arrived at Emory Hall on my twentieth birthday. It caused quite a stir among my friends. The following year he sent me an Elgin American compact in a velvet case for my birthday.

While I was in college, Eric went to New York for the Westminster Dog Show where he was showing Czar, and on his way back he sent me a telegram (I still have it in my scrapbook) saying, "Staying at St. Claire Hotel, please phone." It didn't go unnoticed that he signed this one "Love." I called my mother and asked if I could go to Chicago. She said I could *not*, but all the girls at Ann Emory knew about my feelings for Eric and told me I just had to go. One of them even loaned me her fur coat. So I sent Eric a telegram because in those days you didn't make many phone calls. I still have a copy. The telegram said I'd come. I had never flown in a plane before but I flew from Madison to Chicago and got myself to the St. Claire Hotel.

Eric and Czar, who had just won the Bench Championship, 1947. Eric is wearing the necktie I painted with Czar on it.

I didn't know how to use the dial telephone in the lobby. At home we just picked up the phone and one of two operators, who knew exactly who you were, came on saying, "Number, please." We gave her the three or four-digit number and she'd ring it through. I still remember my grandfather's number was 257 and my uncle's was 422. It wasn't until the '50s that we got a dial phone.

Anyway, I had to ask somebody how to use the phone; that's how naive I was about things. Eric came down to the lobby to meet me. He was having drinks with friends, so we joined them. When he asked what I wanted to drink I said, "Whiskey," trying to sound sophisticated. I didn't know the difference between Scotch and Bourbon; in fact, I usually ordered something like a Singapore Sling that had about seven different kinds of liquor in it. Everybody laughed because it sounded so blunt and crass just to order a whiskey.

Eric had a suite at the St. Claire with a living room and bedroom for me; he had a room somewhere else. We went out for drinks and when we came back he asked if he could spend the night with me. I said yes, but that we weren't going to "do anything". My mother used to say that if you ever went all the way with a man then he wouldn't have any respect for you. We slept in the same bed, but we didn't have sex because I was obeying my mother, despite the fact I had disobeyed her by going to Chicago in the first place.

The second night we went out to dinner and heard a top Swedish nightclub singer, Carl Bresson who sang *September Song*—"...it's a long, long time from May to September...." Realizing how long it might be before I saw Eric again, I was thinking that that night I was going to "do it", but he didn't stay in my room. He kissed me goodnight at the door and told me he didn't feel well. I found out later that he had indeed come down with the flu and had to stay in Chicago several days longer than he had expected. If he hadn't been feeling sick, he probably would have stayed with me. There went my second chance.

I told my mother later on about having spent the night with Eric, but that nothing further transpired. She believed that I was being honest with her.

In my scrapbook are the six-decades-old dried remnants of some flowers I got. There was no name on the bouquet, and I thought they might be from Eric. Years later, I suspected Aunt Viola had sent them, letting me think they were from Eric, and when I asked, she admitted that she had.

Third Chance

Journal Entry, May 28, 1947:

This is the trip I was waiting to make even at the time I had written about my Eastern trip to Connecticut, for the Johnsons moved to California just two years ago—just before I went East. I can remember wishing at the time that my train was going West instead of the direction it took. Well this time my dreams really came true.

Eric and me in Woodland Hills, California, 1947.

The Johnsons invited me to California for a month the summer after my freshman year. My mother was all for my taking the trip.

I took the Santa Fe Chief, and on the train I met two women in the dining car who invited me to have breakfast with them. One of them was Mrs. Schwab from Schwab's Drugstore, famous because it was where all the movie stars went for an ice cream soda at the counter. That's where Doris Day was discovered. Mrs. Schwab was completely into the movie scene and asked me if I had ever thought about being in the movies. I said no, that I had just been in the university. She told me she had an agent she thought I should meet and gave me her phone number at Schwab's, telling me to call her when I was settled at the Johnson's.

The Johnsons thought this was suspicious, so Eric accompanied me to meet the agent who turned out to be legitimate. His name was Ben Medford and he was with one of the top movie agencies. I never harbored any desire whatsoever to act, nor had ever been in a play, but Medford had me go to a couple of studios where I was given a part to read that Claudette Colbert had played from a famous film, "It Happened One Night." At the time, television was just coming in and the movie industry was way down because they were afraid of what was happening with television so there weren't many available parts. It was at that point that Ben Medford suggested I might go into modeling.

I spent the month with the Johnsons at their home on Mulholland Drive and had a wonderful time. Eric knew a number of people in the movie business and we went out to dinner occasionally. We went to movies and several times went to the Johnson's cottage at Lake Elsinore.

It was back to being like brother and sister more than boyfriend and girlfriend. One night when his parents were away, Eric came and sat on the side of my bed and talked with me about nothing in particular. I was so shy that I never said anything to him about how I felt. Sometimes I think, if only I had taken the risk to reach for his hand at that moment, just given him an indication, that's all he was waiting for. In retrospect, I think he was looking for me to give the go-ahead, and because of my age, never wanted to push me.

That was my third, and what would turn out to be my final, chance. Once again, I boarded the Santa Fe Chief and returned to school, more in love with Eric than ever.

College girl, Lake Mendota, University of
Wisconsin with Buffy, Bill's dog. 1947.

Part II

❧

New York: 1948-1951

James Murray's apartment.

I make my modeling debut in The Big Apple, 1948, with a perfect "prop."

⚛ 7 ⚛
Detour to New York

The following January I went to New York, although I was really on my way to California. That may sound strange and as if I didn't know what I was doing, but I had what I thought was a very good reason. I was in love with Eric, but I didn't want to make it look as if I was following him. I thought if I went to New York it would push him to make something happen with me (still unaware that he already had tried). I had no great desire to continue in college since studying art seriously would only prepare me to be an art teacher, and that's not what I saw in my future. I knew I could always paint for my own enjoyment. Having been encouraged by Ben Medford, it was much more appealing to try modeling.

Mother only allowed me to go to New York because I was staying at the Barbizon Hotel for Women. Wisely, she let me go freely, but also left the door wide open to return to Mayville if I wanted. The Barbizon was on 63rd Street on the Upper East Side and had the reputation of being a safe "home away from home" for young women moving to the wilds of New York City to seek career opportunities. It had a doorman, men weren't allowed beyond the lobby, there was a strictly enforced Code of Conduct and Dress, and residents needed three letters of recommendation before they were even considered for residency. Ben Medford wrote one letter; John Thiel, a prominent Mayville attorney, wrote another; the school superintendent wrote the third.

Ben also wrote a letter to Henry Waxman asking him to do a special favor and take photographs of me.

Dear Henry,

Just spoke to my very dear friend, Jayne Blodgett. She told me she was up to see you.

I wish you would do me a personal favor and take some photographs of her for me. I am very much interested in this girl and I think that she will have a big career as a model in New York. I realize you don't want to take every Tom, Dick and Harry and this girl does not have a lot of money to spend. If you would extend yourself it would be of great help making her look good. Please do this for me, Henry, and I will make it right with you.

I expect to be in New York very shortly as I am forming my own motion picture company to produce two pictures and I will let you know when I will be there.

Please call Jayne B. at R 45700 and set up an appointment with her....

Other than a couple of sorority sisters from college who also lived in the Barbizon, I didn't know anybody when I first came to New York. For the first six weeks, once I was home from a day of modeling, I basically didn't go out and even had some meals in my room.

I wrote Mother regularly, addressing the letters "Dear Mother and All," knowing everyone in the family, especially Aunt Viola, would eagerly devour every word. Aunt Viola, who never had any children of her own, called me "Snooky", and I knew I was her favorite niece. I told Mother (and all) every little detail, knowing how interested they were. She kept every single letter and clipping I sent her, which she faithfully pasted into a scrapbook, creating a running commentary of my life in New York. It's from those letters and scrapbooks that many of my memories are sparked today.

Shortly after I got to New York I had my hair cut really short. The agency wanted to do hairpieces with some really exotic looking braids, and I let them cut my hair. Mother was furious when she saw a photo. I had beautiful hair, naturally very thick, dark and wavy with reddish highlights, so I never had to add any color. In fact, I had never before been to a beauty salon in my life.

I started out at John Roberts Powers, but Ben Medford put me in touch with Jackie Copeland, a well-known Conover model, who encouraged me change to Conover. Jackie came from a very good family in Newport News, was married, and lived in Sutton Place, an affluent neighborhood on the East River. She was shocked when she found out I hadn't been out on a date yet, and said she'd call a good friend who had a nice son. Sure enough, Mrs. Schine called me to make the date, and a few nights later her son David phoned to iron out the details.

David picked me up at the Barbizon and took me to my first dinner date in New York at the fashionable El Morocco in the East '50s. El Morocco, famous for its zebra-striped sofas, was (and still is) a popular establishment frequented by the rich and famous—New York's elite socialites, politicians and entertainers. The owner knew David and came over to sit with us. In another room I could hear violins playing, and yet another room had a more night clubby atmosphere.

David was tall, with dark wavy hair and strong, even features. I thought he was very good-looking. I remember on that first date he asked me what nationality I thought he was; I said I thought he was English, which seemed to flatter him, although I had no idea why. I didn't know that Schine was Jewish. He was a student at Harvard and heir to his family's extensive chain of movie theaters and hotels including the

Boca Raton Club in Florida and the Coconut Grove in Los Angeles. The Schines were in negotiations at the time to purchase the Waldorf Astoria.

I liked David. He was sophisticated with an elegant, languid style. Almost immediately, we found we had a lot in common in our political beliefs. He was easy to talk to and had ambition that I found exciting. After dinner we danced a little and made plans to get together again. Then he took me back to the Barbizon and headed up to Boston.

☙

In my modeling career, I was cast into the field of "high-style." I was very tall—five-foot-nine—and able to project an air of sophistication, reserve and exclusivity. Along with modeling, I once tried out for a musical on Broadway produced by Mike Todd, named "As the Girls Go," which called for tall Ziegfield-type showgirls. Joan Blondell was there with Mr. Todd. I had to walk around the stage to the tune of "A Pretty Girl is Like a Melody." I got a callback, but had recently broken my arm so had to to walk around with my arm in a cast and didn't get the part. (Years later, my husband told me if I'd gotten on stage he wouldn't have married me.)

A clipping from *The Mayville News* read:

"...our Conover model Jayne Blodgett, got a big break recently when she was chosen as one of the New York models to appear in the show. Jayne didn't get a chance to participate because she broke her left elbow... she has appeared in several television shows and in one of them she's with Gloria Swanson. Jayne is having a great time in New York and has the great fortune of meeting quite a few celebrities."

I had climbed onto a chair in my room in the Barbizon to swat a fly on the ceiling and fell. My arm hurt, but I didn't think too much of it. Later that night it started to get much worse. The following afternoon I had a date with Harold Rhame, a very polite, pleasant-looking Princeton University graduate, interning in Washington, DC, whom I had met through friends. His father was a doctor and Harold was following in his footsteps. I had been going with Harold for six weeks and when he came to take me out that afternoon, my arm was hurting so badly that we went right over to his father's office where he set my broken elbow. I never had to pay anything for it; he just took care of it.

I was picked for the Miller and Rhodes Fashion Show, which was the top show down in Richmond, Virginia. Fortunately, my cast came off a week before the show. Flying to Richmond was only the second time I'd been on an airplane. We dressed to the hilt for the flight because we had to be prepared for publicity shots when we arrived. The other girls were all top models, but I had never done a fashion show before except a little one for Macy's, so I was scared. During the two days we were down there, we were treated like royalty with limousines that drove us around and special parties in our honor at the country club. I became good friends with one of the other models, Devon O'Leary, who was as excited as I was to go look at historic houses and explore Richmond with the car at our disposal. I absolutely fell in love with the South. As it turned out, Devon was a "friend" of Joseph P. Kennedy, which in retrospect explained why she had money to spend. After we got back to New York, she asked me several times to join her in her box at the races, but I never did make the time to go.

I was once on Gloria Swanson's daily talk show on television for Dumont TV, which was then on the top floor of Wannamaker's Department Store downtown. I was one of the models interviewed and I had to walk across the stage and talk with her. I got a walloping $10.00 for the whole day. Everyone wore brown cake makeup, so they looked like they had a suntan. It was really basic original television. In a large spread in *Parade Magazine*, there was a photo of me with Harry Conover showing how I'm an ideal fashion model, but not good for TV because of my height. Another girl, much shorter than I, in a second photo shows how she was a much better match for TV because the screens were small.

Harry Conover and me in Parade Magazine, *1948.*

One night several of us models were asked to go to Spiro Skouros' party in Mamaroneck to sell chances on a luxury car. Spiro Skouros was head of Twentieth Century, very well known in the movie industry, distinctly nouveau riche, and a very nice old fellow. A huge black limousine, complete with uniformed chauffeur and push button radio on our back seat, picked us up at the St. Regis and drove us out to suburban New York. Mr. Skouros' home was fabulously beautiful, elaborately furnished in the French period, and there were lights strung out all over the grounds, throughout the formal gardens, even down on the beach. His Chinese junk was sailing right out in front of his house in Long Island Sound.

It was an invitation-only lawn party benefit for the Holy Trinity Catholic Church. We sold chances on a Cadillac —a hundred chances at $100 dollars apiece. Priests and executives in the picture business bought chances with $100 bills; in fact, some bought five or six! Just imagine—that was when $100 was more like $500 or $600.

Men wore white jackets, women dressed formally, 'accessorized' with the most beautiful diamonds and furs. The party was comprised of the New York café society and I couldn't help but notice that most of the women were "horsey" looking. Mr. Skouros' brother, the president of Independent Theaters, was there. It was rumored that he had the highest income of anyone in the United States.

The most beautiful buffet supper was served by white-jacketed waiters: heavenly food like ham, turkey, lobster salad, stuffed tomatoes, and gorgeous deserts full of whipped cream and ice cream. I wished my stomach had been bigger because of all the marvelous food wasted.

George Jessel, a well-known actor, songwriter and comedian, drove me and another model home. We dropped her off first, and I thought he was going to drop me off but instead he said, "Let's go get a drink." George was what in those days we'd call "a big wolf"—married seven or eight times—but Ben Medford knew him well, so I figured it was fine. He was a little guy, about six inches shorter than I was, and made quite a play for me. We went to the Stork Club, a well known night club where movie stars, celebrities, and showgirls rubbed shoulders with wealthy aristocrats and powerful politicians. Other clubs drew just the sophisticated or wealthy or sporting crowd, but the Stork Club drew a diverse assortment of glamour, money and power. Everyone made a big fuss about George. When he dropped me off after the Stork Club, he invited me to go to a baseball game the next day.

The following day I met him at his suite in the Waldorf around noon. Eddie Cantor, famous radio star, actor and comedian was there, and all three of us went together. We drove out to Ebbots Field in George's limosine with me sitting between him and Eddie Cantor in the front seat. Never having been to a baseball game before in my life, here I was going to the biggest game of the year between Brooklyn and Boston, with two of the most famous showmen in America. We had a box right by the batters. The Brooklyn team and a lot of other people asked Georgie and Eddie for autographs as the band played, "If You Knew Suzie"—the song they always played for Eddie Cantor because his wife's name was Suzie—and Georgie and Eddie stood up to bow. We were a greater sensation than the ball team. I didn't know it at the time, but we were on radio and I was introduced as Mrs. Cantor, probably because I was wearing dark glasses. We had a police escort and were practically mobbed; people kept shouting, "Hello Eddie, Hello Georgie." George kept making passes at me and Eddie wanted to kiss me every time George wasn't looking, succeeding several times. It was great fun.

Harold said if I went out with George Jessel again he wouldn't go out with me. By that time, I was scared to go out with George anyway, and decided to handle the situation by not answering the phone. Harold and I worked out a system where he'd call and let the phone ring three times, hang up, and call again. I assume George eventually got the message.

CB

When I met Gloria Emerson at Conover, we immediately hit it off. She became my closest friend during my New York years and well beyond. Gloria was a force of nature, a really major and very interesting part of my life. Even taller than I was, she was gangly and unusual looking. Although she had never been to college, she was brilliant. She was also opinionated, impetuous, and melodramatic, an instigator and a chain smoker. Mostly she was ferociously loyal and loving to her friends, especially me.

A descendant of Ralph Waldo Emerson, Gloria had clearly inherited the writing gene, and when she couldn't make enough money modeling, she turned to writing. Eventually, she became the only person ever hired by *The New York Times* without a college degree and one of the few war correspondents in Vietnam.

Throughout our long friendship, Gloria and I wrote detailed, full-confession, heart-wrenching letters to each other. She was a master of the art of letter writing, and I've kept her letters all these years. I'm not sure how she came up with the knickname "Bonehead" or "Boney," but that's how she affectionately addressed her letters to me. We were each other's sounding board and safe haven. We bolstered one another through rough times, shared our dreams and disappointments, and laughed at the absurdity of some of the predicaments we got ourselves into—mostly around men. Gloria always said we should write a book called *Innocents at Home* —the capers of two innocent and naive young women on the loose in New York City in the late 1940s.

It didn't take long after we met for Gloria to sneak into my tiny room at the Barbizon and camp out on my floor for a few weeks until the management found out. I could hardly plead innocent, so she and I began making plans to find an apartment together. We found one on 66th between Madison and Park, an upscale neighborhood where we later found out Bernard Baruch, elder statesman and advisor to presidents from Harding to Truman, lived across the street.

Ours was a typical sub-street apartment, down a couple of steps with a terrace in the back, a tiny kitchen and a slightly less tiny living room. To spiff it up, we painted the floors. For days, we couldn't get to the bathroom without crawling across the top of the kitchen cabinets. The oil paint took forever to dry, so finally we got fed up and put newspaper down, which of course stuck because the paint was still tacky. After pulling up the newspaper, we had New York's most literary floor!

cs

Once when I was returning from Mayville on the Pacemaker, the train that went between Chicago and New York, a man said hello as I walked by. When I went into the dining car for dinner, the maitre d' sat me at a table for two and the same man came and sat opposite me, introducing himself in a thick foreign accent as Bela Kornitzer. He told

me later he had asked the dining car steward to purposely seat him there. I remember him telling me I had a profile like a Roman coin, which I took as a compliment. The next morning when I got back to the Barbizon there were a dozen roses from him and an invitation to dinner. Since I didn't

Douglas Fairbanks, Jr. and Bela Kornitzer (on the right).

know anything about him, I asked Gloria to go along.

Bela was unusual and turned out to be a very interesting man. He was Hungarian and had been a prominent journalist in Budapest before he came to America in 1947, fleeing first the Nazis and later the Communists. Here, over time, he reestablished himself as an influential journalist. He was most interested in the success stories of Americans and did many interviews of prominent men. He believed that "the best way of learning about a nation is to talk to the people on their home ground when they are in their slippers and you can get the unaffected personality ... not the carbon cliché of the press agents." Wanting to show how American democracy begins at home with family-instilled principles and ideals, he focused on father/son relationships and domestic life in order to get an honest and different angle about America's leaders. That made Kornitzer stand out as a writer. He wrote a book called *Fathers and Sons* for which he interviewed all the Eisenhower men.

When I met Bela he wasn't famous in America yet. He was just an interesting man who knew many important people and was charmingly European. He kept asking me out, and I took Gloria with me for most of our dates; in fact, he and I only went out a few times alone. One time when we were with Gloria he asked me to marry him right in front of her. Of course, I declined. I was seeing David and Harold and was not interested in marriage yet.

By then I had met Francie Stone through David Schine. Francie was a mainline Washingtonian, nine generations back on both sides, transplanted to Nonquit, Rhode Island and New York. Francie was a dynamo. She became my mentor and hired me to work part time as her Gal Friday when I wasn't modeling. Old enough to be my mother, she took both Gloria and me under her wing, treating us like her own daughters.

Francie had spent her childhood all over the world, much of it in French department stores. Athletic, she became district doubles tennis champion with Marianne Newbold, won swimming races, sailed all kinds of vessels from sloops to yawls, and often attended the yacht races at Cowes off the Isle of Wight.

In her twenties, she decided she wanted to work for Macy's. When they asked if she could speak Italian she replied, "Of course," as if she just assumed everybody did. For the next few months she slipped out at lunchtime and got an Italian pal to translate for her. She wasn't able to eat, but she was at least able to keep her job and started the promotional department at Macy's, now a famous personal shopping bureau. She added 150,000 customers and was always racing around town delivering things that hadn't arrived on time.

During World War I, Francie was organizer and National Director for the Netherlands-America Foundation, an organization dedicated to strengthening the bonds between the people of both countries through exchanges of arts, sciences, education and public affairs. She had married Charlie Stone, an architect who designed some of the monuments and buildings in Washington. They had a son named Lanier who was a student at Yale at the time. I remember being impressed by her telling me how Lanier, when he was only two, had fallen through a skylight in their six-story house in Georgetown. He hit the landing four floors down and was found by his grandmother, just sitting there, only somewhat dazed. I thought what a lucky person Francie was.

Francie was the kind of person who "motored" places; she didn't *drive*. "Let's motor up to Nonquit," she'd say. She had a convertible car; back then convertibles had little windows in the back where the top folded up. It was impossible to have a big window because they didn't have plastic folding ones back then, so visibility behind was hampered. She invented a window that had an adjustable frame, which she called "Safety Sight." One of the reasons she wanted me to work for her was that she thought I could go to the embassies and sell the ambassadors windows for their convertibles. She didn't make much money on the windows, but I had fun driving her convertible around town.

A few months after I met Francie, she told us about an apartment that her best friend, Helen Coolidge, President Coolidge's granddaughter, was subletting. It was on Mitchell Place near 49th Street and First Avenue where the United Nations is now. It was a much better location than our current apartment, so she helped us get it. The apartment was on the third floor in a building with a doorman. It was small—basically one room with a Murphy bed, a dressing room, bathroom and a little kitchen—but it was elegant. Beautiful tapestries and paintings hung on the walls and there was even a fireplace. A little door led out onto the fire escape balcony, and we could look down into garden apartments below. One of us slept on the Murphy bed and one in the dressing room—cramped quarters, but a great address, plus it had the convenience of the cross-town bus right there

Gloria in our apartment on Mitchell Place.
1949.

on 49th Street. It was luxurious. In order to afford the $150 per month rent (which would be the equivalent today of $3,000), we ate meals for 25 cents—mostly canned spinach and peanut butter. Although the rent was expensive, we were much more concerned with where and in what style we were living than what we ate. We also ate out much of the time because we had many dates, and in those days women never dreamed of paying for anything.

In all the years I knew her, Gloria never once came to Mayville. My mother was always a little suspicious of her, thinking she was taking advantage of me because as long as I had a place to live, Gloria could always be sure she had a place to live. I guess I was like a security blanket in a way. She was usually borrowing money from me, which my mother didn't like, but I didn't care. Gloria may not have been the most steady person to have as a roommate, but she was loads of fun and we were really close friends. We lived in that apartment for eight or nine months and got plenty of mileage out of our time there.

It was in that apartment that I made dinner for Jack Kennedy when we first started dating. Gloria was having an affair with Langdon Parker Marvin, III, whose father was a law partner of Franklin Roosevelt's and a Navy commander in World War II. Langdon lived in Washington during most the time Gloria and I were living together in New York. He had been a roommate of Jack Kennedy's at Harvard and was still one of his best friends. Gloria and Langdon kept pestering me to have a date with Jack.

I wasn't particularly interested in meeting some congressman named Jack Kennedy, whom I knew nothing about, plus I had my hands full, going with both David and Harold at the time. Finally, however, I agreed to a blind date with Jack, but only because Harold was interning at a hospital down in Washington and had invited me to a party at his club, so I thought I'd kill two birds with one stone. I told Harold I'd come to the party, but couldn't be there until 11 o'clock.

Gloria and I took the train down to Washington and were met at the station at around 5 pm by Jack's chauffeur, who brought us back to Jack's house. Langdon was already there, as was one of Jack's sisters. I had been told by Gloria and Langdon not to talk about the war or any kind of sickness because they said Jack had an incurable illness. Langdon knew about Jack's Addison's disease, which had been covered up successfully by the press. We had a fun dinner, went out dancing for a while, and I was aware that I was somewhat interested in Jack. Then I popped over to the club to have my date with Harold, whom I was loosely engaged to.

Gloria and I returned to New York, and I began to hear from Jack mostly via telegram and phone calls from trains. I started going out with him. So I was seeing David Schine, Harold Rhame and Jack Kennedy, but I was still really in love with Eric out in California.

David Schine and me at the Waldorf Astoria, 1948.

≪ 8 ≫
The Libertarian with a Chip on His Shoulder

F or over a year I went with David, in fact, right up until the time I was married. He was in his senior year at Harvard and started flying down from Boston to take me out, then began to send me plane tickets so I could fly up there.

One weekend after we had been going together for a while, I went up to Boston for a football game. David lived in Elliot House at Harvard in a very nice apartment with a fireplace. They weren't supposed to have girls upstairs but he smuggled me in. That night we drove through Connecticut and stopped at a hotel in the middle of the night; I still have the key to the room. Then we drove on down to Stockbridge to visit his little brother at boarding school and back to Boston so I could fly back to New York. That was when I really started going with him seriously.

David was heir to a family that owned a large chain of hotels and theaters and was worth a fortune. He modeled himself after Howard Roark, the main character in *The Fountainhead* by Ayn Rand. Roark was the epitome of an independent-minded man, and David was one of these people who wouldn't compromise on anything. He got me to read *The Fountainhead* and *Atlas Shrugged*, both of which made a great impression on me. We were very much in sync in our feelings about being libertarian—believing that the moral purpose of one's life was to pursue your own beliefs and that the only social system that meshes with this morality was laissez-faire capitalism, less government control, and more individual rights. This made David extremely anti-Communist and very conservative. His ideas reinforced much of my thinking.

David, at age twenty-one had all these plans that he shared with me—how someday he was going to have a magazine like *The Reader's Digest* that would be distributed all over the world in different languages, and how he would be able to influence people. He was very serious and mature for his age, very proper, but also very insecure. When we went to the 21 Club he told me he was concerned they wouldn't let him in because he was Jewish. He had a real chip on his shoulder. Probably because of that, David liked to pull rank and flaunt his wealth; he threw his name around and had all his clothes custom made. He'd just call somebody up and suddenly we could go to a movie or to Radio City Music Hall. He'd just ask for the manager and we'd get escorted in because everyone knew who he was. One night we went to a hotel where Tommy Dorsey was playing; during a break, Dorsey came to our table and invited us into his office to talk.

David had a Cadillac convertible with a telephone in it, which was quite unusual in those days. He thought it was great; he'd stop at a stoplight and pick up the phone. People looked over and saw him talking on the phone that looked just like a regular telephone, and he loved seeing the expressions on their faces. He also had one of the first three Polaroid cameras because his father was backing Dr. Land, and a portable voice recorder that he took to class to record lectures.

In one of Gloria's letters she says that David was "... so exciting...he's such a paradoxical person you can never tell what's going to happen next...." That just about summed him up.

David had the feeling that he was being followed a lot. It's possible his father might have been having him followed, but he also tended to be insecure and paranoid.

I knew his friend, Roy Cohn who would figure prominently in David's life in the next few years. David and I occasionally went out to dinner, tennis matches and swimming at the River Club with Roy.

In January of 1949, he wrote me a touching note after we had had a little disagreement:

My Darling Jayne,

Never did I love you more than I do now—you have just hung up on me and it sounded as though tears were in your eyes. I would have loved to have spent this weekend only with you in Boston. If I had only felt that I wasn't imposing on you to make you travel so far alone and to monopolize your time, after all, you have told me you are a very popular persona and what of the Hungarian and Amherst princes and am I being fair to you when I make you unhappy and give you a conscience that bothers you. I wish I could see you Saturday but I guess you don't want to see me anymore. Just remember if you ever change your mind... .

I don't think you'll call me back tonight so I am going to sleep. It is with a smile on my lips and in my heart—a smile for you make me very happy because I love you and I believe you love me too!

David

❧

I met David's family when they invited us to dinner at the Wedgwood Room in the Waldorf Astoria Hotel, which they were negotiating to buy at the time. Throughout the whole evening, his father only said a gruff hello and goodbye to me in his thick Latvian accent; he just sat there making it obvious that he didn't approve of me. David's mother was very pretty, asked me a few questions about where I went to school and proceeded to tell me about how she had her shoes made to order. David's parents came from Gloversville, New York, where many Latvian immigrants had settled and worked in the glove business. When his father was young, he had hitchhiked across the country to Hollywood and eventually the family started buying theaters, a hotel in Albany, North Hampton, Los Angeles and Miami. Once David and I went up to the North Hampton Inn where everybody waited on us hand and foot, as if we were royalty.

Towards the end of dinner, David's parents asked him to leave the table with them and I was left with his sister, her escort and a girlfriend. When they came back after forty-five minutes, David was very quiet. We said our goodbyes, and left. David and I continued to see each other after that but I think his parents were afraid he was going to marry me; they didn't like that idea because I wasn't Jewish. I don't remember how many months went by until David started saying that he couldn't get married at this age, but he'd always take care of me—whatever that meant. I was seeing him practically until the time I got married.

Three or four years later he married Miss Universe, who was Swedish. I saw him only once briefly after I was married, but certainly was aware of what was happening in his life when I received a call from the government in 1954 during the Army-McCarthy Hearings.

From The Mayville News, *1948. "Mayville's Conover model, Jayne Blodgett, is seen in this photo wearing a little number that nicks the bankroll for $3,800."*

9
The Loose Cannon

D *ear Mother and All,*
The formal I got was $69, one I can wear in
winter and I will pay for it myself with checks.
Harold knew I was going to see David and even drove me to
the airport. Then my flight was cancelled so he took me to
the train, called this AM from Washington. Guess he loves
me so much nothing else matters....

I liked Harold's intelligence, but he was a bit of a hot-head—always so insistent—which I attributed to the fact that he was my age. He felt so young to me, which was part of the reason I was always attracted to older men. I just wanted somebody more established and steady. It bothered me that he was a little shorter than I was, so I had to wear flat shoes, but he was highly intelligent; I knew he was going to make a very good doctor.

Harold's parents lived near Prospect Park in Brooklyn, and when he took me home to meet them and his brother, I liked them immediately. His mother was from Georgia and I liked the fact that she was very much DAR, Colonial Dames, and a member of the Daughters of the Confederacy. She had a bit of a southern accent and was very sweet and kind. His father was a lovely, gentle person. I became very fond of his parents and enjoyed going with them to their beach club out on Long Island, a pleasant change of pace from the hectic life of Manhattan.

Budding doctor, Harold Rhame, 1948

Harold got very serious very fast and kept pressuring me to get engaged, but the more he pushed, the more I kept making excuses. I didn't want *not* to see him but I didn't want to get engaged and drop everybody else. Although he knew I was seeing David, he didn't want to stop seeing me and I thought I could manage him. David didn't mind that I was seeing Harold. So both knew I was dating the other, but it came to a head one evening when they overlapped due to too-close timing.

I had a date with Harold, and David was coming later. I told Harold that I could only see him for a short time and I was furtively trying to get rid of him before David got there. Finally I got Harold out and a few minutes later David arrived. When David and I went down and got in a taxi, Harold, who had apparently been waiting outside, followed us in his car down Park Avenue and whizzed past us through a red light. He was really angry, and it occurred to me that if he had had a gun he just might have used it to shoot David— or me!

Of course I was telling my mother and Gloria all this. Between the two of them—Mother worrying because Harold was so intense and Gloria giving constant input about what I should do—that I became anxious. I think if I had been left on my own with nobody advising me I might have handled it more gracefully.

Photo by Jim Widmer.

✂ *10* ✂

Jack Kennedy's Blue Jeans

Shortly after Jack and I met on our blind date, he sent me a telegram from Palm Beach saying, "Wish you were here. Can you go out Saturday night when I come back to NY?" He sent a telegram asking me for a date! Occasionally he called, but often he just sent a telegram.

One of the reasons Jack and I got along so well, I think, was because we had both experienced being sick in our childhoods, and had spent so much of that time reading. We had both read many books and had fun comparing our favorite childhood stories. Even more important, we could empathize with each other about being bedridden as young children. That was something that definitely made us compatible, plus I was always interested in politics.

Jack was extremely thin and had a yellowish cast to his skin, which I attributed to the Atabrine he had to take for malaria. The Navy gave it to everybody who was in the Pacific during the war so they wouldn't catch the disease. Although he was tall, he was also very lanky and bony and weighed less than I did.

I found this photo of Jack at a thrift store a few years ago. It shows what he looked like when I knew him. I tried to find the photographer but couldn't.

It never occurred to me that Jack had the potential to be president of the United States because he never came across that way at all to me. We talked about books and politics and he was fun to be with, but he always seemed kind of boyish despite being ten years older than I. He was not at all serious, and I wrote my mother, "...he has this little boy quality that makes me feel motherly." At the time I was seeing Jack, he didn't have much ambition. It was his older brother Joe who had been groomed for politics. Joe had been the apple of his father's eye, and Jack hadn't expected to be the one running for office. When Joe got killed, Jack knew he was next in line, and he wasn't that pleased. He really wanted to be a college professor, I think, and would have liked to live a less pressured life.

It was famous among Jack's group of friends that he never carried any money. He just didn't seem to think about details like that, but somehow the bill always got paid. He constantly had a crowd around him—usually a group of old school friends—and some guy would inevitably pick up the bill. I always wondered if they were reimbursed. This group of admirers was at his beck and call, all agreeing with him, fawning over him, all hoping to get things from him. I'm sure they were thinking that if they could get a job through the Kennedys, they had their careers made. It was always like that when Jack and I went out.

Jack was very casual about everything. He could go to the 21 Club and have an expensive dinner like blinies with caviar or to Howard Johnson's and have a hamburger and a milkshake. It didn't really matter to him. In fact, in a book called *The Kennedys* by Peter Collier and David Horowitz they mention, "One girlfriend of the time, Jane [sic] Blodgett, remembers..." and they go on to say about how casual he was about things. I was interviewed by one of the authors (I can't remember which) at my home in Bedford. I was supposed to send them copies of all these letters I had telling my mother and Gloria about Jack, but somehow the letters had gotten wet and blurred so I couldn't send them. I never talked to the authors again and the book was not published until 1989.

Once Jack called from Washington to ask me out to dinner. For some reason, I wanted to cook for him and told him I'd make dinner at my apartment. Of course, I told my mother all about it:

Jack Kennedy flew up Friday night to see me, had wanted me to come to Washington but came up instead because I promised to cook dinner for him. Got a small chicken for $1.10 and quartered and then browned it in a skillet. Then I made fresh asparagus in a double boiler and had half a recipe of baking powder biscuits and half a packet of ginger bread mix served warm with ice cream. Very good. Got a mixed green salad and put mayonnaise on it. It wasn't too difficult and turned out well except the asparagus wasn't quite well done and the chicken not salted quite enough but then I had never ever attempted a dinner before. I'm learning a lot in this apartment, it is good training for me. Jack was surprised and said, "I didn't think you had it in you." We went next door to the cocktail lounge on the Beekman Roof and then to the Wedgewood Room at the Waldorf, where Morton Downing is entertaining—he's a good friend of Jack's....

I remember that evening at the Wedgewood Room. Morton Downing put the spotlight on our table and said, "Oh, Congressman Kennedy is here." He then proceeded to make a couple of jokes, including one about Jack being so tight that he even saved string. Then he came over and sat at our table.

On about our third date, we had artichokes for dinner. I didn't know it at the time, but I was allergic to them and when we got in the taxi, I had to open the door and throw up onto the street. I was totally embarrassed, but Jack was casual about it and thankfully never brought it up again. Needless to say, I went immediately back to the Barbizon.

After several weeks of dating, Jack asked Langdon how he thought he was doing with me, probably figuring Langdon would have heard things from Gloria. He wanted to know what my feelings were about him. I was still going out with David and Harold. Jack would sometimes call from the airport and want to know if I was busy that night or available to go out with him. Then he'd disappear for a few weeks and I wouldn't hear from him, but he'd always resurface.

In May, Jack invited me up to Hyannis Port for the weekend. According to Gloria, that was because he could corner me up there. Gloria said, "Now don't sleep with him if you want to marry him." I didn't have any intention of sleeping with him. I knew his friends Torbet MacDonald and Charlene Edwards were going to be there also. (Torbet had been captain of the football team at Harvard and Jack's roommate; several years later he would take Jack's seat in the House of Representatives when Jack was elected to the Senate.) Charlene was supposed to fly up with me in the family plane, but since it was already being used, Jack bought me a ticket on a commercial airline, and Charlene got there somehow on her own steam.

I took a cab from the airport to his grandfather's house in Boston. I remember telling the cab driver to take me to Honey Fitz's house. The driver was surprised, I'm sure, to be taking me to the home of the former Mayor of Boston. Jack was waiting for me there, and we drove down to the Cape. He had his arm around me and was kissing me as he was driving.

We finally got to the house around midnight. I remember the huge flagpole on the front lawn. The house seemed endlessly spread out—at least nine bedrooms—and very casual. Torbet and Charlene had already gone to bed, so there I was alone with Jack. We went into the kitchen where there was a huge white frosted cake in the center of the table, and Jack asked if I wanted a piece. We talked a little and then kissed goodnight, nothing new since we had done a lot of kissing before, but never anything more. I had one of his sisters' bedrooms, which I knew because there were clothes in the drawers with her name sewn in. I got into bed, and all of a sudden Jack walks in my room with no clothes on. "Well," he said. "I couldn't sleep. Can I get in bed with you?"

By then, of course, I wasn't going to say no.

When I came down for breakfast, I thought people would already be down, although we didn't really settle the night before what time everybody was going to wake up. I was alone, since Jack hadn't stayed all night with me. I was waiting in the library, and the butler came and brought me coffee. Going through the library, I found a few books that I always wish I had stolen. One had a whole dedication to his mother, written by hand. I remember reading it, and when Jack came down, I remember talking to him about it. There were autographed pictures all over the library—the King and Queen of England, Winston Churchill, Harry Truman, and Franklin Roosevelt among many others. There was a big painting of the USS Kennedy, a ship named for Jack's brother Joe.

Dear Mother and All,

I was more or less the hostess, being Jack's date so sat at the head of the table. I was served first. Dinner was by candlelight and we had turkey, demitasse in the living room.... I wore my English suit and your cape.... I like Jack very, very much but he is very strange. He was on a PT boat [my mother wouldn't have known who Jack Kennedy was then] *during the war and was lost on a raft for days. The only chance for rescue was for one of them to swim and Jack did; he was in the hospital for months and had typhoid and is almost as thin as Bill, which he is very sensitive about. He has my idea of a voice that's a combination Boston and southern accent. He has most appealing little boy characteristics although he is very brilliant, graduated cum laude and has written several books—*Why England Slept *and* My Brother Joe.

The letter continues:

... but he's very quiet and serious, makes no effort to be entertaining. He is always just kind of relaxed. He has a strange appeal. I'm always the one who has to make conversation, which is difficult. He is very close to his family, in fact, Langdon says the only solution for the Kennedys is intermarriage.

Jack and I took a long walk on the beach in the morning, with him swinging a stick as if he had a golf club. Later, we went horseback riding at the stables with Torbert and Charlene. I borrowed Jack's blue jeans from his time in the navy because I hadn't brought pants along. None of us, especially Jack, were good riders except Charlene. I had ridden a pony on a farm only a few times, but I always liked horses and wanted to learn more about riding. Jack's father had just gotten an Irish jumper and we dared Jack to jump the horse. He had a bad back, which I didn't know about then, and probably shouldn't have even been on a horse, but he took the horse over the jumps, not just once, but *six* times. I always thought, *Wow, he's a guy who takes chances that aren't too smart.*

Jack's jeans were too tight on my thighs and split when I was riding the horse. Thinking I'd mend them and give them back, I took them home, but since I didn't own another pair of jeans, I often wore them around the house and even used them for painting. I never remembered to give them back and still have them wrapped in tissue paper in one of my drawers. That's how I came to have a pair of our 35th president's blue jeans.

Jack and I were going somewhere that day and went to the garage to get a car. The garage at Hyannis Port was full of cars to choose from, and I immediately noticed a brand new Cadillac convertible. Jack didn't say anything about the new car; he probably didn't have any idea what was there, but he certainly didn't say anything like, "Oh, there's a whole new car!" as somebody else would have. He was totally matter of fact. We got into this convertible and he didn't have any idea how to put the top down nor what all the different buttons were for.

That evening, we all sat on the floor of the living room and played games. I remember the doorbell rang, and it was a couple of his cousins who came in and visited for close to an hour. I got the feeling Jack was irritated that they had stopped in. He was also annoyed that I beat him in Chinese Checkers; Jack didn't like to lose at anything.

The letter goes on:

We spent a quiet weekend walking on the beach, playing catch, sitting in the sun. Played Chinese Checkers last night ... It was too cold for swimming although yesterday was beautifully sunny. I offered to go to church with him and he said, "Oh no."

Many years later when I got into real estate, Helen Ginnel said in one of our ads that I was one of their top brokers and could beat Jack Kennedy at Chinese Checkers.

ᛒ

I have a book, *The Dark Side of Camelot* by the investigative journalist Seymour Hersh, published in 1997. Hersh interviewed Gloria about Jack; these are excerpts from his book with Gloria's observations—eloquent statements that really give an impression of what Jack was like.

The writer Gloria Emerson was an aspiring journalist when she was first introduced to Kennedy ... at a cocktail party. "I was almost hypnotized by the sight of this man... he was such a stunning figure; he didn't have to lift a finger to attract women, they were drawn to him in battalions, by the brigades, and the interesting thing was he didn't care if you made an effort to make him interested in you. He was perfectly cordial, but come and go, it didn't really matter to him. Kennedy... always seemed to be surrounded by men and they were always talking about a strategy or the moves of other people. It was rather mysterious and exciting. You, of course, as a young girl were of no importance whatsoever. Jack always called you 'kid' because he couldn't remember women's names. It wasn't just the looks, it was the sense of mockery and that kind of fierce intelligence. He didn't like people who babbled, he was very impatient and often very tense. I didn't realize it then but I think he must have been in pain a great deal of the time."

The book goes on to say:

Emerson was dating one of Jack Kennedy's classmates from Harvard when she and Jack met—it was before his marriage to Jacqueline Bouvier—at the inevitable round of weekly parties. She said, "He was totally unselfconscious; he walked around half naked with just a towel wrapped around him, all bone, all rib, all shank. You have to have tremendous self-assurance to do that; I've never met anyone like that again. It was the audaciousness, the intensity, the impatience, even the bruskness. Here was a man who wasn't going to wait. He was going to get what he wanted, he was going to go from the House to the Senate to the White House and that was quite thrilling."

This is a reference to me:

"Another part of his charm... was young Jack Kennedy's total indifference to his own beauty. He didn't care if a woman said 'yes' or a woman said 'no,' there would be another one. He was so absent minded about the women he was having affairs with. Once I had a roommate in New York when we were both very young; she was having a

very pleasant affair with Jack and not taking it too seri-ously which seemed very wise to me. But he could never re-member her name... [which is not true, because he did. I had told Gloria that the first time he came to my apartment he said, "Hello, kid, how are you?"] *and he couldn't figure out how to get in touch with her* [that's because he didn't know my last name that first time] *and so he had to describe the woman so the doorman could identify her."*

Jack had about the biggest absentee record of anyone in Congress at that time, and Langdon and other friends al-ways joked about it. This is a great paragraph about Jack from one of Gloria's letters.

Dearest Dearest Boney,
I meant to tell you about Jack, as you know he went out to the coast supposedly to attend some conferences with some big wheels from the airlines regarding LP'S bill [Langdon had a bill that he was doing for air merchant ma-rine separation of subsidy from air mail pay]. *Well, he hasn't done, as you well know, a blessed thing except leer at Anne Blithe, my God, and lie on the beach thinking. Well,* The Boston Post *came out with a big article saying he was wast-ing the taxpayer's money and he was a loaf and a playboy, etc. Langdon told me all of this, he was just delighted and the article was really something. Well Jack got word of it and sent great cables to his Boston office to do something right away so they applied great pressure on another newspaper to come out and say that Kennedy was just kill-ing himself attending thousands of conferences to further his Air Merchant Marine Bill and was at the point of col-lapse from all the work he had done and Boston should be proud of their young, eager, for what I wonder, very indus-trious congressman. Well, Langdon and I almost died laughing and I thought you would be interested in hearing about it. So I made some copies of some of these things.*

I remember going shopping once with Jack. We had lunch at Howard Johnson's after having spent the night together, and then went to Saks Fifth Avenue because he needed to get some shirts. We walked though the store and he never even thought to ask me if I wanted something. He had no sense of giving to anybody and was not thoughtful in that way. He had all these shirts that were made to order; I remember the price was something like $49 a shirt (equivalent to about $400 today!). I was thinking *this is the most fantastic price to pay for a shirt*. He didn't seem to have any sense of money and didn't appreciate what he had, probably because he had never had to work for anything before.

One night Jack and I were staying at his suite in the Waldorf Astoria. The phone rang and it was Jack's little brother Bobby downstairs in the lobby. He wanted to come up for a moment to speak to Jack, so I had to hide in the closet, freezing cold, with no clothes on while Jack talked to him for a few moments.

When I was staying with him sometimes and he'd be writing a speech, he'd give it to me to read, wanting to know how I felt and to get my reaction to it. He knew I was a reader and that I had great respect for language.

Jack and I dated in 1949, the summer before I got married. People ask me if I was in love with Jack Kennedy and it's a difficult question to answer. I had mixed feelings about him: I wasn't in love with him, not as I was with Eric or David, but I would have married him if the circumstances had been different. I was taking our relationship in a matter of fact way and basically didn't feel he was ready to marry. I knew he was seeing other women, which wasn't an issue to me since I was seeing other men. I was aware that Jack was a playboy and loved the thrill of the chase. His style was to go in and out of people's lives, and I wasn't about to wait around for him. He could fall in love easily, but he was calculating about who he'd marry, and I knew there were several reasons why he probably wouldn't marry me. One, I wasn't Catholic.

Two, he was very interested in marrying someone in the Social Register, which I was not in at the time.

I didn't fall for Jack like other women did. I knew I probably could have played it to make him want to marry me, but I also felt it would have been a disaster. Charming and irresistible, he ultimately wasn't particularly romantic. He was very light hearted with this little boy quality, almost like a teddy bear, but not really a man yet. I wanted a man with drive and serious intent, someone with his eye on a target, inspired. That's what I was drawn to and at the time I knew him, Jack wasn't that way. He liked to play the field, and to him women were playthings. I wanted someone more serious and above all, I wanted emotional security.

Sometimes I imagined what it might have been like to marry Jack Kennedy. Gloria always said that marrying into the Kennedy family would have been awful; that Kennedys should only marry each other because they are so tightly knit that anyone else is an outsider, but it certainly would have been a very exciting life.

After I was married, Gloria and Langdon visited the Kennedys at Hyannis Port. She had never been there before, but Langdon took her up there. Joe Kennedy, Senior had a reputation for making passes at Jack's or anyone else's girlfriends, even when Rose was sitting there. One night there were all these people at the table; Gloria got up to go to the powder room, and he followed her in and put his arms around her.

Jack didn't know when I got married because a month or two would go by when he wouldn't be in touch. He wasn't a thoughtful person in that way. Eventually he'd resurface, and apparently when he couldn't find me at my old phone number he asked Langdon what my new number was.

Gloria wrote me:

... the kid [meaning Jack Kennedy] *is still single. He asked Langdon what your telephone number at Mitchell Place*

was. Typical isn't it? Langdon told him you were married and abroad and said he looked terribly crestfallen. I was furious at Langdon for not saying something about what a very <u>desirable</u> husband you have and what a thrilling honeymoon you were having. But the kook, despite my previous coaching on what to say....

Modeling shot, 1948.

❧ 11 ❧

The Lonely Hearts Club

I met my husband-to-be at one of Francie Stone's famous cocktail parties for the "Lonely Hearts Club," a corny, tongue-in-cheek name because it was hardly that. Francie knew everyone you ever wanted to know in New York, so it was a logical way for people to expand their social horizons. The parties were held in the latest luxurious hotel suite that Francie always managed to live in, and were "bring your own bottle." They weren't like a singles gathering; they were more just a lot of people, some of whom already knew each other, meeting and intermingling with other people. Of course, Francie never missed an opportunity to introduce people she thought might be perfect matches.

It was a very hot summer day in 1949, and I went with Harold, who Francie knew I was engaged to. James Murray, a good friend of hers, was there, and I'm quite sure she meant for me to meet him, despite—or maybe because of—Harold.

Jim's entree was to read palms. He read mine, but I don't remember what he said. He was pleasant looking, quite a bit older than me and seemed sophisticated, but I didn't think much about him other than that. I mingled with others and left on Harold's arm.

I didn't think enough of James to wonder if he'd call me, but Francie had something else in mind and was the kind of woman who persevered. My mother had sent me a fur neck piece—a couple of animal skins fastened together and worn like a scarf—and Francie was adamant that I needed to have it insured. Since Jim was an insurance broker, she called him and suggested he write the insurance policy for my fur piece. Under pretense of discussing an insurance policy, he called to invite me to dinner at The River Club, a prestigious private club on the East River.

That was in October and we began to see each other regularly. It was also around the time I got the diamond ring from Harold so was now seriously engaged. Harold was chomping at the bit to set a date in June to get married in Mayville. He wanted a big, showy wedding, which I wasn't anxious for, not to mention I really wasn't in love with him.

Jim was twenty years older than I. Well traveled, established and mature, he had the kind of worldly knowledge that interested me. He had good taste and was very savvy about all sorts of things, which impressed me. My father had been much older than my mother, so whether through genetics or through acquired taste, I was more comfortable and secure with older men than with those my age.

Modeling shot. 1949.

❦ 12 ❧

Dear Mother and All

I had been juggling David, Harold and Jack—quite involved with all three, engaged to one—and by the fall of 1949 I had added Jim to the mix. Eric was always in the background. I had seen him briefly when he called me on his way back from a visit to Sweden, and I met him and his younger brother Alan at Grand Central Station for lunch. I would have left everyone to marry him because he was my one real love. Ironically, he was the one I never really had an intimate relationship with.

When I think back to this period—which I admit probably sounds insane—I have to remember I was only in my early twenties, hadn't really dated in high school or college, and had barely had the chance to discover who I was in relation to men. It was an era when there were very few options for women other than marriage.

The letters I wrote my mother and those Gloria wrote me only *begin* to explain that time. In retrospect, it's quite funny, but at the time it was very traumatic. One day, almost twenty years later, I took all the letters to work and read them to Helen and the other people in the office. They were practically rolling on the floor with laughter.

Here's a letter about a fairly typical weekend and the rather frenzied level it reached.

Dear Mother and All,

.... Expected to spend such a quiet weekend and really didn't, drove to Morristown with George Bramson Friday night, Saturday to the Atlantic Beach Club with Harold. Saturday night dances etc., very lovely place and private beach cabanas and their own bars, chaise lounges, etc. I just went in and got wet, didn't swim, got a nice tan, however. Had dinner at the Blue Spruce Inn on Long Island, very nice. Sunday I slept late then went up to the hospital to see Harold, having nothing better to do, got back around 9:30 to find that Jack Kennedy had been calling madly from Boston, that David had come and waited an hour to see me. I got in touch with Jack at the Waldorf and couldn't reach David so went out with Jack. Saw David Monday; he'd flown down from the lake with Stig Holtz, his Danish friend. Went out with David last night to the Beekman Roof for a drink, showed him our roof and the neighborhood. And then had dinner at Billy's little club. Went with David to Huntington Hartford's penthouse apartment at the River House. We arrived in the middle of a formal dinner party and he took us around his apartment showing us his extensive painting collection.

And another weekend:

Dear Mother and All,

It will be a quiet weekend after all, really for once, unless David comes down from Boston, which I doubt. He has his last exam Saturday and has gotten B's. We had a fight last night so don't know what will happen, he's been so difficult lately. ... Jack Kennedy called me last night. He was at the New York airport on his way up to Hyannis and would have stopped over if I had gone out with him but I had a date with Harold who was already here, darn it, I was so disappointed....

Harold got away from the hospital Sunday night. I spoke to David on the phone and Jack Kennedy came for bachelor dinner. He called just after Harold left so I saw him also today, he was working on a speech to give for graduation class and wanted me to read it and give him my comments. I drove him to the airport before where he caught his plane back to Washington. He certainly is an enigma....

Jack Kennedy came in Sunday night from Miami... I was out with Dick Collin. He expected me to be in when he called so I fooled him.

David tried to get in touch with me Sunday evening and Monday and of course I was out with Jack but I really wanted to be out with David. ... he went back yesterday afternoon ... called in the evening from Albany about coming to the Stork Club for dinner but I didn't have a dress to wear for summer evenings at the Stork and El Morocco ..... Later that night Jack and I had dinner at 21.

Jack had stayed over for a wedding in Oyster Bay of Gladys Pulitzer's (of the Pulitzer Prize family) granddaughter, but came back and took me to 21, telling me he left the wedding early because he would rather spend the time with me.

That was the night I drove him out to La Guardia in his rental car and got lost driving the car back through the seamy Upper West Side of New York. In those days it didn't bother me much to have that kind of thing happen. I had the car the next day, so Gloria and I drove it around and then I dropped it off at his father's office on Park Avenue, hoping his father was going to be there so I could meet him. He wasn't in, so I just returned the keys to his secretary.

Harold is busy at the hospital, which he hasn't been able to leave for a week. He calls every day and David called last night. I don't know where Jack Kennedy is this weekend but I'm not worried because he'll call eventually—he's just that way—but he asked Gloria what she thought of our romance and wondered what his chances were with "The Kid" [as he called me].

David got back from Florida last night and stopped by the store this AM. Also called tonight. He's with his family as they now have an apartment at the Waldorf Towers.

Had dinner with Jack Kennedy at 21 Friday night. Had dinner with Jim Murray last night and saw "Madame Bovary"—excellent picture. Tomorrow night I'm going to his cocktail party and Thursday night to the ballet with Harold.

By now I had been seeing Jim for about six weeks, and he was saying *let's get married; we've got to get married; I want to get married.* He told me he was making reservations to go to Europe, and if I didn't marry him he'd go alone.

Finally, exhausted, I retreated to Mayville for Christmas to regroup and try to make up my mind. I had Harold's engagement ring and had left Jim with the idea that we were getting married. I sent a telegram to each of them from the airport in Milwaukee, saying "Love you and miss you." I remember the woman who took the information started laughing because I sent the same telegram to both.

It was a terrible time for me because I didn't want to hurt either of their feelings. Neither knew I was debating which one to marry. I admit I was feeling quite insecure. I had a deadline because Jim was going to leave in March, so I had to get married before that if I chose to marry him. I just panicked; I could have decided not to marry either Harold or Jim, but I couldn't imagine going back to New York and living like this or starting a whole new life. I also didn't want to return to live in Mayville. I just wanted to get away from it all. I thought, *I've got to get married.*

Of course I was receiving letters of advice from Gloria.

Dear Bonehead.

I just got back to Philly last night around 11 and couldn't have been more pleased to find two letters from you in my mailbox. And they were such wonderful letters; for once I know exactly what you've been doing. Your life sounds very peaceful. After your slaving so and juggling all the crises all winter, I should think you should be on the verge of collapse. I howled when I read how you were drooling for some social life and that people out there were still mad for Monopoly.

Speaking strictly for myself, I think you should stay in Mayville for a long while to think this mess out. There is no reason why you should have to get married to anyone at all. But I do realize that you are anxious for various and sundry reasons, so proceeding on that track I think you would be happy to marry Fred. It is certainly nice to know he still loves you... [I had gone to dinner with Fred Karston who I had dated in high school, and he didn't notice I was wearing an engagement ring. Then he wrote me a long letter saying how embarrassed he was that I didn't tell him I was engaged.]... *and I am very curious to find out what he says when you tell him of your engagement, only to whom are you going to say you're engaged? He is the best bet—young, attractive and tall, obviously wealthy and a boy from a similar background. But if he doesn't propose and even if he did, what would your mother say? Then Jim is the best bet.*

Darling, except for the fact that I love you dearly and want you to be happy, it's really not my concern who you marry. But if I were you I would certainly positively unequivocally choose Jim over Harold. Harold has been very nice and I am not mad anymore about that awful Friday night and I realize he is intelligent, ambitious, popular etc. but you will have to work for five years and he will be gone most of the time at the hospital and you will be in a strange city and you have always hated the fact that he is shorter.

Well, Jaynie, you can't even be together for an hour without quarreling; you two are just not compatible. While Jim is very intelligent, more social, can give you five times as much materialistically, adores you in an adult way and is more attractive to me any day... Just because he wants to go by freight [meaning the freighter that he was proposing to go on for our honeymoon] *is no indication that he doesn't have as much money as he says, he has a gorgeous apartment, belongs to two very expensive clubs, has a car* [which was somewhat unusual for someone living in the city then]. *Both Bob Wright and Frankie have referred to that. I can understand why your mother would be annoyed and worried, but only you can handle that. Too bad she couldn't meet Jim or perhaps he should write her to calm her down, anyway stress Harold's drinking, temper, etc.*

After Christmas I made excuses to Harold as to why I wasn't coming back to New York yet—that I had a sick relative or something like that. Jim flew out to Mayville and when he returned to New York he called every day, talking for an hour on the phone, which was a lot in those days. He was a great talker on the telephone, which I found really very flattering.

Dear Bonehead,
I was disturbed to read that your mother is somewhat confused about your engagement and I can only repeat what I said before, that Harold knows about Jim Murray and is aware that you might become engaged to him. I might see him [Harold] *New Year's Eve in DC. I hope not, as you know I have no desire to see him now more than I have to and will write long details of what he might say. I really think this situation is getting out of hand and you will have to take decisive action now and not wait until you get home. Write Harold, tell him you think you would be unhappy together and that you could not help him with his career or*

social life. Really Bonehead, you simply must do something immediately! Keep me posted on what goes, Gloria

Finally, I broke my engagement with Harold by writing a letter. I was afraid to see him and tell him in person since he could get very intense about things. It was very difficult not only because I didn't want to hurt Harold, but also because I loved his mother and father, and didn't want to hurt them. His parents had been expecting me to be back for Christmas, and when I left for Mayville they didn't have any idea I was trying to make up my mind whom I wanted to marry.

I was twenty-three. Everyone I knew was married except Gloria, because in those days most people, both men and women, married that early. Women didn't have a lot of options, so needed security. It's just what we did in those days.

Gloria wrote:

Well, Lamb Chop this will be my last letter to you in 1949. It has been a dreadfully wonderful year and I don't think there will ever be one just like it for either of us. I guess we're wiser, sadder, brighter older girls and we certainly do have some unforgettable memories. Regardless of what I'm doing at the strike of twelve this Saturday, let it be at the Chevy Chase Club in Washington or the University Club or the Sulgrave [an exclusive private club], *as soon as someone yells "Happy New Year" I'm going to close my eyes for half a second and say, "Hello, dear Jaynie" and "Happy New Year." I mean that and you do the same; we'll establish mental telepathy.*

All the love this side of the Mississippi—Glo Glo

March 4, 1950. Our wedding day at Alma and Ham's house.

❧ 13 ❧

Marrying Into the Eccentric Murrays

S o I decided to marry Jim Murray. All "my other men" would resurface after I was married—Jack in 1953, David in 1954, Eric in the late 1950s, Jack again in 1961 and Harold in the late 1960s.

When I returned to New York (not letting Harold know I was back), I moved into Jim's elegant bachelor apartment on 81st Street on the East Side, and he stayed at his club. It was in a townhouse built in the late 1800s, one of the beautiful granite ones, not a brownstone. It was a one-bedroom apartment that had a large living room with high ceilings and rich wood paneling from floor to ceiling, wonderful built-in bookshelves and a fantastic huge stone fireplace. Jim had comfortable sofas and two big club chairs that would travel with us everywhere we moved, and interesting tables made out of a Revolutionary War drum cut in half.

Mary, Jim's maid, came every day. She was from Yugoslavia, had been with him several years, and stayed on with us until we moved to the country.

Jim came from a rather unusual, and not particularly close, family. His father James was fifty-five when he married Alma Van de Bogart who was only twenty-four, and they had eight children: Bronson, Alma, James, Peyton, Janet, Archibald, Alex and Hamilton. The Murray family was considered a little eccentric among the rest of the relatives. There's a passage in a wonderful book entitled *For My Children,* written by Jim's cousin Barbara Moray, in which she says, "He [Jims' father] married very late in life a high-minded person who worked in the Y.W.C.A. They had a large family, no money, and the children turned out mostly to be very odd and wild."

According to Jim, his father was one of those old New England patriarchal types—very stern with his children and not a particularly warm person. He had been a lawyer and began having children late in life. Severe and staunchly religious, he donned a black frock coat in the morning and sat in his library all afternoon writing books on religion. A devoted Presbyterian, he was very involved in the Moody Bible Institute, which provided evangelical training so people could proselytize in their everyday lives. Every summer there was a Moody Bible retreat in a big hotel in Northfield, Massachusetts, and Mr. Murray moved the whole family up to a farm he owned nearby in New Hampshire. Every Sunday the Murrays attended church services and Sunday school at the Moody retreat. Back on the farm, Mr. Murray made all the children go pick bugs off the potato plants and sleep outdoors in tents on wooden platforms. He was a fresh air nut and thought it was healthy, but his children hated it.

Apparently, Mr. Murray had lost a lot of money in real estate in New York City. His brother Archie was much more financially successful, and his sister Olivia had married into great wealth, so she paid for all her nieces' and nephews' educations in addition to leaving them quite a sum of money.

All I really know about Jim's mother was that she was mildly overweight and had trouble with her feet, but the family never said much about it; in fact, they were very close

The eccentric Murrays and guests in the dining room of Aunt Olivia's East 71st and Madison townhouse: far side of table, 4th from left Jim, then Alma, Ham; head of table Olivia Cutting, her husband Bayard to her left; Jim's mother to the left of Bayard. 1930s.

mouthed about it. The condition passed down to three of her sons including Jim and unfortunately, down to our daughter, Jaynie. It was a fairly mysterious condition in which the nerve wrapping gets twisted up in the nerves. When a person with this condition got a cut or a blister, it didn't heal and they could get infections very easily. Jim got an infection in his foot when he was playing baseball at the age of eighteen, and because his ankle never healed completely, he couldn't stand on it very well.

He was supposed to go to Princeton, but because he needed to see doctors regularly in New York City for his foot, he ended up going to Rutgers, which was closer. When I married him he had crutches, but I didn't learn much about the condition until we were on our honeymoon. Then he told me how two of his brothers had inherited the problem, which they thought came down through his mother's line. Back in the 1920s, Jim's brother Bronson got a blister on his heel and died within a week when he was at Dartmouth College.

His brother Peyton, who lived on Long Island, had a couple of toes amputated.

Alma, the older sister, went to Smith College, married Hamilton Fish Potter who was a descendant of Peter Stuyvesant, and they lived in Smithtown, Long Island. The Potters were lots of fun, and often came to Bedford for weekends. Alma always affectionately called our children "bambinos."

Then there was Janet whom her siblings always treated like their "weird sister." Janet went to Vassar, was always very sweet to the point of syrupy, but really sincere. She was one of those very religious people whom you know actually mean it. She never married, and was always taking care of the rest of the family. Scholarly and not very practical, she did research down at Princeton, knew Albert Einstein, and was into 14th Century literature and Gregorian Chants. Aunt Olivia Murray Cutting had seen to it that she was always taken care of, so Janet never seriously had to work. I was nice to her, and when we moved to Bedford, I invited her out often, but my husband's "male chauvinist" attitude toward her bothered me.

I didn't know about Jim's younger brother Alexander until we were on our honeymoon. He had been a star basketball player at Yale, then gone into the service and apparently had a nervous breakdown, supposedly because of his unrequited love for Governor Averill Harriman's daughter. He was discharged from the service for medical reasons and had simply disappeared. Nobody in the family but Aunt Janet ever bothered to look for him. I remember once asking Jim how he could have a brother and not try to find him? That was unheard of to me. Anyway, Aunt Janet finally tracked him down in a hospital out on the West Coast and brought him back to live in a halfway house near her on Long Island.

Jim's brother Hamilton had married when he was eighteen, divorced very young, then married again later. I met him at our wedding, but didn't know him very well until later when his children were all grown.

The farm in New Hampshire was still in the family when I married Jim and I suggested that he go look at it. He decided to have some selective lumbering done. It took a long time for the family to finally agree to sell it, and by then it was falling apart. They also had a farm down in southern Illinois run by a tenant farmer bit it didn't make any money for them. The ten Murray cousins involved were holding onto it because they could never agree on what to do with it. The tenant farmer could have been walking away with everything since nobody in the family watched over it.

⅋

The picture that appeared in the newspapers to announce my engagement looked as if I didn't have anything on under the fur piece that my mother had given me. My shoulders were bare but I was actually wearing the brown strapless dress I had bought for $85 back when I did a fashion show at Macy's. I wrote my mother that I hoped the picture wouldn't hurt my chances of getting into the Social Register and that I bet everyone at home thought I was a regular Bobo Rockefeller (a prominent and scandalous socialite at the time).

All Jim's brothers and sisters except the long lost brother who lived on the Bowery came to our wedding.

We were married on March 4, 1950 at Alma's in Smithtown by her husband Hamilton who was a Justice of the Peace. My mother was the only one from my family at the wedding. Bill couldn't make it because he was at the University of Wisconsin and it was right in the middle of the school year. Gloria was my maid of honor and, of course, Francie came. I got married with all this confusion around David and Harold, and was constantly worried that Harold would suddenly appear brandishing a gun. All went smoothly, however, and the wedding party headed back into the city for the reception in the grand living room of Jim's apartment. Over a hundred people, including Jack and Gertrude Astor, Jack and Edie Chrysler, and Jack's brother, Walter Chrysler attended. Just before the guests arrived, Crowley the butler built a fire in the big stone fireplace. He lit it before remembering to open the flue, so the room began to fill up with smoke. Everyone had to run around opening windows before the guests arrived.

L-r: Mother, me, Archibald, Jim, Hamilton Potter, Gloria Emerson.

The announcement in *The New York Times* read:

Ms. Jayne Blodgett, daughter of Mrs. William Morris Blodgett of Mayville Wisconsin and the late Mr. Blodgett was married at noon today to James G. Murray of New York, son of the late Mr. and Mrs. James B. Murray, at the home of the bridegroom's sister and brother-in-law, Mr. and Mrs. Hamilton Fish Potter of Smithtown. Mr. Potter is a Justice of the Peace. The Justice of the Peace performed the ceremony. The bride, who wore an informal afternoon costume [that's because the mayor of New York had married Sloan Simpson who was a well known model and she wore a navy blue suit so I thought I needed to wear a navy blue suit which was kind of "in" at the time] *was attended by Ms. Gloria Emerson. Hamilton Murray of Havertown, Pennsylvania was the best man for his brother. Mrs. Murray was graduated* [actually, I only went for two years] *from the University of Wisconsin* [Madison]. *Her husband attended Riverdale Country School and was graduated from Rutgers* [he didn't actually graduate].

Syndicated gossip columnist Nancy Randolph wrote:

... the romance of the tall beautiful brunette Jayne who left a small Wisconsin town a few years ago to make her mark in Manhattan reached a story book climax in her marriage yesterday to James Gordon Murray of New York Social Register.... The bride, daughter of Mr. and Mrs. William Blodgett, was well known in the field of high fashion. Her unusual height and air of reserve lent the desired atmosphere of exclusiveness to the gowns and furs in which she posed sometimes for magazines like Vogue. Her husband of 43 of Yonkers, NY, Mr. Murray, was previously married to the former Jane Porter Breed of Baltimore.

How fortuitous that Jim's previous wife had the same initials as mine, so all the towels and pillowcases I inherited had the correct monogram for me!

After the wedding, we went up to Marian Frelinghuysen's country home in Lennox, Massachusetts in the Berkshires for a few days since the freighter that would take us on our honeymoon wasn't due to depart quite yet.

Dear Mother and All,

Mary [Jim's maid from New York] *was here when we arrived and had a chicken roasted and everything ready. It's a charming place called a rustic farmhouse but quite complete with four baths, electric kitchen, dishwasher, etc., maid's room and nursery on the third floor. It's all done in charming French provincial manner with off white carpet, very gay prints, wall papers, etc. One bedroom is done in a bright yellow. Our bedroom has a huge bed like Jim's but soft, lovely down comforters, pink linens, soft aqua and pink wall paper. There's a beautiful view of the Berkshire Mountains across a valley and about fifty acres of land....*

...Two feet of snow, wonderful air, I'm getting lots of sleep, took some pictures today, also took a walk by myself [my husband didn't get up in time] *and broke a window by throwing a snowball at it* [I threw a snowball at the window to wake him up, thinking it was funny] *which made Jim a bit angry. I guess he didn't want to tell Marion that I did that. We had to get someone to come and replace it.*

Jim, around the time I married him.

Isle of Capri, 1950.

⚘ *14* ⚘
Honeymoon Over the Atlantic

*J*im, a passionate world traveler, had planned our honeymoon as a great adventure—a brief excursion into North Africa followed by a jaunt around postwar Europe in a car loaned to us by friends. I had never been out of the United States and couldn't wait. He had booked us on the Hav, a Swedish freighter that had been a cargo transport during the war, but now carried passengers along with its freight. During World War II these cargo ships, called Liberty ships, traveled in convoys to bring supplies for the war effort. They were built fast and furiously in US shipyards from one single design intended to last only about five years. Luckily, I didn't know this at the time.

Traveling by freighter was quite a chic, new thing to do and just beginning to become popular. A cargo ship was allowed to take twelve people or fewer; any more and there would need to be a doctor on board. One of the conditions when shipping on a freighter was accepting that things changed often, that you never had an exact time of departure; you had to be flexible and ready to hop on board in twenty-four hours or less.

The trip across the Atlantic was to take fourteen days —leaving from New York, crossing due east, passing through the Straight of Gibralter, stopping briefly in several North African ports, then heading north across the Mediterranean to Genoa.

Things changed. The port of departure was shifted to Boston, so we took the night train and boarded the Hav in Boston Harbor. Instead of going directly across the Atlantic, we hugged the coast, passing Cape Hatteras during the Ides of March—always considered a dangerous time off the coast of North Carolina. Rerouted, we landed in Cuba where the captain told us we had four days before departing. Jim had spent his first honeymoon in Veradero Beach at a gorgeous seaside resort run by Margarita LaRosa, one of the daughters of the vice president of Cuba; he knew I'd love it. We jumped on a small plane and flew across Cuba, spending an idyllic couple of days (despite my very bad sunburn) on the lovely rustic beach, sleeping in a thatched roof hut.

The Hav was as good as, maybe better than, a luxury liner. Our cabin was large with port holes on three sides. A steward and stewardess were available to us, and Jim had arranged to have breakfast served in our cabin every morning. At every other meal we sat with the captain, the officers, and the other ten passengers. Anytime you wanted, you were welcome to go in the galley and pilfer the refrigerator.

It was like a chapter out of the novel, *Ship of Fools*, because there was such a cross section of people on the boat. With only twelve passengers and intimate quarters, we had nothing better to do but get to know each other well. There was even a little dog aboard, the ship's mascot, who contributed to the camaraderie.

I remember the model and photographer couple going to Istanbul, hired by *Life*. We played canasta with them every night and got so close that we saw them while they were living in Stamford after we moved to Bedford. There was an elderly Italian gentleman from Brooklyn who was going back to Italy to see his relatives whom he hadn't seen since the war. A lovely young Jewish woman and her sister from Boston were returning to Casablanca. Later we learned that they always traveled on this boat because she was having an affair with the captain, a very attractive younger man.

Setting out from Cuba, we ran into a terrible storm in the middle of the Atlantic—massive waves crashing over the rails and slamming the decks. I've never been so sick in my life, but finally got some Dramamine. Luckily I didn't know then what I learned later, that those ships were known to break in half, having been thrown together in a hurry and not very well built. Later there was a scandal involving Henry Kaiser who had made a ton of money during the war, building the ships way too fast, using substandard materials. Thankfully, I was blissfully unaware of that fact as I groaned in our cabin.

Eventually we outran the storm and continued toward Africa. We passed the Canary Islands, and on Easter weekend landed in Casablanca, Morocco's chief port, where we spent four days. Casablanca had been an important strategic port during the war and the site of a huge American base, which was the staging area for aircraft headed for the European Theater of Operations. In 1943, Casablanca had hosted the meeting of Churchill and Roosevelt as they discussed the progress of the war.

Five years after the war, Casablanca was mainly native Arabs. It was very exotic, especially going through the Casbah, the walled, older part of the city. Its narrow winding streets were crowded with people—the women all in black—and amazing smells, some enticing and others not so—including what was floating down the gutters. We took carriage rides to navigate the city and ate dinner at some lovely hotels. We were even able to take a tour of the Palace of the Shah where his wives lived, where his children had their own palace, and where the gorgeous gardens were kept.

The Hav was anchored way out in the middle of the harbor since it drew too much water to dock at a pier. When we wanted to go off the ship, we had to climb down a metal ladder and board a launch, which took about twenty minutes to get to shore. If we stayed out late at night a guy would row us back out to the Hav in a little boat with just one light in the front and sidle up alongside the freighter so we could scramble up the ladder.

We wanted to take a bus to Marrakesh where I was eager to see La Mamounia, the famous hotel where Winston Churchill liked to go on vacation, set up his easel and paint. But we never made it there; we were told it wasn't considered safe or predictable, that the bus would be loaded with natives and their chickens, and that we might not get back in time because our captain couldn't tell us exactly when we'd be leaving for Algiers.

Algiers, the capital of Algeria, was at that time still a French city and quite different from Casablanca. As we approached, its white buildings seemed to just rise out of the Mediterranean. The modern part of the city sits on the level shoreline while the ancient part creeps up the hill. We stayed in the same hotel where all the chiefs of the armies congregated during the war when the French were fighting in Algiers.

From Algiers we went to Tunis, the capital of Africa's northernmost country, where Jim almost missed the boat. We had been in the *sooks*, the Arab quarters, and it was time to get back to the Hav. I went ahead and got on the boat, but Jim, being the bargainer he was, wanted to finish haggling for a very rare prayer rug. The Hav was preparing to leave, in this case from a dock, not out in the harbor. The captain said he couldn't wait much longer; he'd give him another ten minutes. Everyone was lined up on the railings, waiting for my husband to come down the long wharf. Finally the captain said we were going to have to leave without him and asked if I wanted to get off the boat or stay? I said I'd stay; all our things were in our cabin and I couldn't just leave. Jim would have to get some other transportation across the Mediterranean and meet up with us in Italy. Just as I had made that decision, I heard the whole boat cheering. I looked out and there was Jim running up the wharf at the last possible second with the Persian prayer rug rolled under his arm!

It took a day to cross the Mediterranean and land in Genoa where we spent one night and then hopped over to France to pick up Jim's friends' car. The Ledouxs had left it

Biarritz, France.

in storage while they were back in the States, and we were free to use it for a month. It was a yellow Ford convertible, and we certainly stood out everywhere we went. Everybody knew we were Americans and when we drove through towns, people would wave and say *Viva la Americano!* We drove around Italy for almost a month. Jim, being in the insurance business, constantly worried that since the car was a convertible, people could rob it very easily. We couldn't lock all our luggage—and we had plenty—in the trunk. We had at least six big suitcases because my husband took his tuxedo, dress shirts, etc. I had a couple of evening gowns, plus we had heard that Europe was still short on soap, Kleenex and toilet paper, so we brought our own. Part of the way through our trip, realizing we had over-packed, we sent half our luggage back to the United States.

Five years after the war, people were just starting to come back to Europe on trips, but there was still plenty of damage to be seen. There was leftover bomb damage to buildings and the remains of ships wrecked off the shore of Normandy. In England there was still rationing, and on the mainland, people were looking for American cigarettes, candy bars and things like that.

We visited Lake Como, a breathtakingly beautiful part of northern Italy. There we stayed at the world famous Villa d'Esta and spent a couple of days looking around, buying silk scarves and "dressing gowns." We then drove to Venice, down to Bologna and into Tuscany where we made a special stop at La Foce, which was owned by a relative of Jim's, and has a very interesting story.

Piazza San Marco, Venice. My purse was made from crocodile skin smuggled out of Cuba.

Iris Origo was Jim's Aunt Olivia's granddaughter. She was officially a different generation from Jim but only four years older, so Jim and Iris thought of themselves as cousins because they were close in age. It gets complicated because Jim's father married a woman twenty-eight years younger than himself.

I had met Iris briefly before when she came over for a family funeral in New York. She was born Iris Margaret Cutting. Her father was William Bayard Cutting, the son of Olivia and Bayard Cutting, a rich railroad and banking financier. Her mother was Sybil Cuffe, the daughter of an Irish peer. After Sybil and William were married, they traveled all over the world, particularly in Italy, and had only Iris. Sadly, when Iris was eight, her father died of tuberculosis while they were in Egypt.

Sybil and Iris settled into Villa Medici di Fiosole, a fabulous villa just outside Florence. In 1924, Iris married Marchese Antonio Origo and the newlyweds moved to a rundown villa, La Foce, that they bought in southern Tuscany in a valley known as Val d'Orcia. It was an incredibly barren area and the farmers who lived there were totally impoverished. Antonio and Iris dedicated their lives to helping improve the land and everyday life there. They brought in an irrigation system, started schools, a hospital and many other things, financed by Iris's grandparents, Olivia and Bayard Cutting.

In 1925 they had a son, Gian ("Gianni") who died of meningitis at the age of eight, breaking Iris' heart and sparking her to embark on a writing career to cope with her grief. Much later, during the war they had two daughters, Benedetta and Donata.

Before World War II began, the Origos were working with the government developing irrigation and agricultural techniques. Mussolini visited them at La Foce because he was interested in agriculture and wanted to learn what they were doing so successfully to turn the desolate land into arable land, which helped the local economy and could therefore help Italy.

During the war, instead of fleeing to some safe haven, the Origos stayed at La Foce and cared for refugee children, many brought from Genoa and Turin to escape the fighting. Iris helped anyone attempting to escape Facism—local people, escaped prisoners of war, partisans, anyone who was trying to get through the German lines, or peasants simply struggling to survive. As the Germans prepared to occupy La Foce, Iris fled with sixty children on an eight-mile march over a mined road under shellfire to get to the relative safety of the town of Montepulciano. She documents this story with emotional immediacy in her book, *War in Val d'Orcia*.

After the war, Iris and Antonio divided their time between La Foce and Rome. Although we knew Iris wouldn't be at La Foce, Jim and I wanted to see it, so took the drive out to Val d'Orcia before heading to Rome where we had dinner with her and Antonio.

We returned the car to the Ledouxs in Milan. From Milan, we took the Orient Express over the Alps into Switzerland, and then on to Paris where Jim, resigned to the insecurity of our luggage, bought a Jaguar convertible. We spent a month driving around France, then crossed the English Channel on a car ferry to England and Scotland.

In Scotland we visited Selkirk, a small town near the southern border, in search of the Murray family homestead, Phillipaugh. It was the first time Jim had been there. We found the cemetery at the Kirk (Church) of the Forest, where members of the Murray family are buried along with maternal ancestors of Franklin D. Roosevelt whose ancestors also came from that area. The plaque out front says, *"Here lie the maternal ancestors of our 32nd president."* So, my children are actually related to the Roosevelts.

Jim and I basically had a wonderful time in all our travels, but there were a few incidents that set off arguments. I realized this showed a tendency in Jim to feel threatened by other men in relation to me, which I found very upsetting. In

The 1940 Jaguar, which we drove around England and Scotland and shipped back to the US. We sold it before we moved to Bedford.

Capri I bought a black silk swimsuit, which they made overnight. (Imagine making a swimsuit!) When I put it on, Jim said it was cut too low and that he wouldn't pay for it unless they put a larger piece in the cleavage area. I wasn't going to have a man tell me that; I fought back, so we had an argument but eventually I gave in.

We also had an argument in London. A good friend of mine named Peter Finnegan had been sent to New York from London by his family to train at Macy's. He said if I got to London on my honeymoon to come into Finnegan's Department Store and ask for him; that I could buy cashmere sweaters at a cut rate. So I did just that, buying three or four. I remember Jim and I had a big fight; my husband was convinced that I was romantically connected to Peter Finnegan despite my assuring him I was not.

We were supposed to be going to a cocktail party that evening planned by our friends the Davies in our honor. They had invited some duke and duchess along with a few other people they wanted us to meet. I was so angry about the argument regarding Peter that I said wasn't going. It escalated into a battle of wills, definitely not physical because my husband was always very much of a gentleman, but really unpleasant. Anyway, we ended up going to the party, but by the time we got there all the friends they had invited to meet us, including the duke and duchess, had already left. It was rather traumatic and embarrassing.

I remember another time Jim got angry when we were on our honeymoon. We were driving around somewhere in Europe and when a train full of soldiers went by, I spontaneously waved at them. It was perfectly innocent. Whenever soldiers came through Mayville during the war, we'd all go out and stand and wave. Jim got furious, and I couldn't fathom why that made him so angry.

Because our crossing from the US had taken three times as long as expected, it pushed the rest of our trip up and we returned in August instead of May. We were booked to come back on the Caronia out of South Hampton and almost missed the boat—again! In Scotland we had bought a couple of antique tables. We were the very last people at the very last minute to run up the gang plank carrying the tables, all the other passengers standing at the rails watching as the Caronia readied to depart without us. Later, people asked us if we were the ones who came on with the tables and had held up the departure. Overloaded with extra things we had bought, we became kind of famous.

The Caronia was brand new, one of the first ships built after the war, and one of the smaller liners. It was a British line, White Star-Cunard, and we were lucky to get passage because it was almost sold out. Although we went first class, our cabin wasn't as big as our cabin on the Hav and although the Caronia was very luxurious with swimming pools and three dining rooms, it wasn't anywhere near as much fun as the Hav. The intimacy of life on the Hav— getting to know the twelve passengers, the captain and crew— was a world apart from being with so many people on the Caronia. We sat at the captain's table coming back only one night, whereas on the Hav we sat with everybody every night. The way over was more like going on a camping trip; the way back like staying in a resort.

On the return trip there was another huge storm in middle of the Atlantic. Actually, the entire voyage back was worse than the way over on the Hav as far as my seasickness, even though we were in first class cabins. When I put water in the bathtub to take a bath, I could see the water sloshing back and forth, which immediately made me seasick.

What was supposed to have been a two months' honeymoon ended up to be four-and-a-half months, but neither of us was complaining. I loved *almost* every minute of it.

Part III

❧

Bedford: 1951-1993

Photo by Hal Phyfe, one of the main society and theater photographers in New York. 1952.

∞ 15 ∞
Country Wife and Mother

After our fabulous adventure abroad, we came back to the elegance and luxury of Jim's apartment in New York. Mary was still with us, and occasionally we employed Crowley, the archetypal movie butler with the archetypal name. The son of Aunt Olivia's butler, Crowley did all the bartending whenever we had large cocktail party, and Mary made and served the hors d'oeuvres. When we had a dinner party Mary did most of the cooking. On a normal day she came in the morning, usually served Jim breakfast in bed, but I cooked dinner. I hadn't done much cooking since my mother had not been very patient with me in the kitchen when I was growing up, but after I was married she sent me recipes that I wanted to learn how to cook. Once I started, I really began to enjoy it.

Having given up my modeling career, I didn't have any income. I wanted some money of my own to buy a few household things because I felt uncomfortable always having to ask Jim for money, so I decided to get a job. I went to

Bonwit Teller and was hired on the spot to be a salesgirl. When I got home and told my husband, he said I couldn't have a job, but that he'd give me an allowance. He couldn't possibly have his friends see his wife working in a store. So I had to call Bonwit's and get myself fired before I even started.

Whenever I bought something for the house—paint or wallpaper or something like that—Jim loved it because I did the painting or hanging of the wallpaper myself. He didn't mind at all because I wasn't spending any money on the labor and I always did a beautiful, although not always meticulous, job.

Because of his bad foot, Jim was used to being waited on, especially being served breakfast in bed by Mary. I was trying to discourage the habit because it really bothered me. He'd have breakfast, then be on the telephone and wouldn't get going to his office until about 10:00 in the morning. I got really antsy about his getting up and going.

Jim had been on crutches a lot on our honeymoon and was actually very fast. He had been able to ride horses and do just about everything except dance, which never really bothered me because I didn't like to dance; I never thought I was very good at it. After we came back to New York we went to his doctor, Dr. Hamilton Southworth, who was one of the top doctors in New York at the time. He had been trying to persuade Jim to get his leg amputated below the knee for a long time, but Jim was understandably resistant. I was able to persuade him to do it because a prosthesis would enable him to walk much better.

He had the operation at Doctors' Hospital in New York, performed by Dr. Patterson, the top surgeon in the city. After about six weeks he was fitted with a prosthesis, which he had to learn how to use. I remember having a fight with him because he was not using the prosthesis; he reverted to the crutches, and I was anxious for him to get off the crutches and walk. I was really angry with him; I think I even slapped his face once, which made him sit up and take notice. Once he started learning how to walk with the prosthesis, he got very good at it and even learned to dance well. For the next forty years he was able to walk normally.

Jim's apartment was a lovely place to live, but not a good place to raise a family, so we began looking for either a larger apartment in New York or a house in the country. I wanted a river view, so we looked on the East River, hoping to find an apartment with a terrace overlooking the river. The River House was lovely, and we came close to buying a fantastic apartment there, but it didn't have an elevator and I had begun to think of baby carriages. The thought of going up and down stairs with baby equipment was daunting.

Simultaneously, we were looking at houses outside of New York City. My mother was encouraging us to get a house, thinking it was much safer being in the country because of the not-unfounded fear that an atomic bomb might be dropped on New York City. The Cold War was still hot, especially with the added fear that the Soviets might have The Bomb and could be trigger happy enough to drop it on a big city like New York. People possibly within range of radioactive fallout made shelters in their basements or hired a company that specialized in digging holes in back yards for shelters—tax deductible, of course. The shelters were stockpiled with water and enough cans of Spam, peas, and Campbell's soups to tide a family over until the radioactivity theoretically dispersed.

So, ultimately we decided to move to Bedford, which was around forty miles outside New York City. Bedford in 1950 was definitely the country, and I loved it because it reminded me of Mayville even though it lacked a river. It was still very rustic and absolutely beautiful with big old trees, rolling hills, dirt roads and many horse riding trails.

We rented a house for a year and then bought the house on Guard Hill Road, which went right through the center of Bedford Village. Apparently, George Washington's troops used to ride through there, and General Washington would tie his horse under an oak tree, dating back to the time of Christopher Columbus, that still stands at the edge of the village. Most of Bedford had been burned down during the Revolutionary War.

Bedford was comfortable because it was more old money than new; people there were inclined to have tattered, museum-quality rugs rather than modern wall-to-wall carpeting. The town oozed Colonial history, which, being a history buff, I just loved. One house dated back to 1690 and sat right on the road, which is how they built them in those days. Our house was an 1830s renovated Colonial with five bedrooms and a maid's room in the back. We eventually made the root cellar into a bomb shelter and later put in a swimming pool.

Jim bought the house in his name only, and I went along with it thinking that was what a wife did. My mother was much more of a liberated woman and didn't think much of my husband for doing that.

We moved to Bedford in January and Jaynie was born in November. Mother came out and stayed for about a month after she was born to help me. I had Olivia fourteen months later and James two years after that, so I had three children within four years. I nursed all my children for at least six months, which was not done very much in those days, but my Uncle John the pediatrician was an avid proponent of it.

After we moved into the Guard Hill Road house we started getting *au pair* girls from Europe, which could be done very easily through agencies in New York. One girl, Gwen, was from England and had worked in Buckingham Palace for Queen Mary. She stayed with us for about four years and was almost like a second mother to James—actually, quite disconcertingly possessive.

After two years in Bedford, we gave up our membership at the River Club in New York because it was too much driving back and forth to parties. In those days people were not as careful about drinking and driving; everybody thought it was still F. Scott Fitzgerald's time.

Jim was the typical '50s father, not like many fathers are today. It wouldn't have occurred to him to change a diaper or feed the baby. When the children were old enough to go to school, I was up early to get them ready. On Saturdays and Sundays, Jim tended to roll out of bed by 9:00 or 10:00. He wasn't someone who got out and played much with the children. I admit I didn't expect him to either, probably because my father hadn't been inclined that way; he mostly sat and read when he was home. Back then, fathers didn't get out and play baseball or games that much with their children unless they happened to be particularly the type of person who wanted to. By the time we had Jaynie, Jim was already forty-five, so maybe he wasn't feel-

L-r: Olivia, me, Jaynie in Bedford, 1954.

ing very energetic, or maybe it was because his father hadn't played with him, so he had no role model. Also, my husband probably would have been more athletic if it weren't for his foot.

On weekdays, Jim commuted into New York on the 8:30 train, which was luxurious with a club car and porter who served coffee, tea and biscuits—very English. It was divided into sections, men on one end, wives on the other. Husbands could go sit with their wives, but women didn't sit in the men's part. No liquor was served except at Christmas and New Year's.

Jim was a real city boy and had never lived in the country except for those New Hampshire summers he preferred to forget. He wasn't at all handy about things; he could hardly even hang a picture. I remember once I was painting the kitchen and he started out helping. I looked at him and he was wearing his good shoes, which got totally splattered with paint. After a few hours of doing something like that he was just not very enthusiastic, so was not a good person to ask to help. We got a big lawn mower that you could ride on; he'd mow, but I was always on edge, wondering if the grass would get too long, especially if we were having guests for cocktails or dinner. I wasn't fussy; I just wanted the lawn to look well-kept.

CB

James' Christening; l-r: Bill, Olivia, Mother, James, Jaynie, Margaret. 1955.

Raising children in Bedford was wonderful in many ways. We had six acres with plenty of room for the children and dogs to run around, trees to climb, and the pool in the summer, which friends loved to come splash around in. I had suggested to Jim that if we put in a swimming pool we could help pay for it by renting the house out some summers, and he agreed. Two of the people who came to look at it were singer/writer Margaret Truman, the daughter of President Truman, along with her husband Clifton Daniel, a reporter for *The New York Times*. The one question she asked was how was the drinking water? She didn't end up renting our house, which was fine with us because she had two rambunctious little boys.

Exceptional parental involvement contributed to the schools in Bedford being some of the best in the country. I wanted to expose our children to as much as possible, so before Kindergarten I had all three enrolled in play groups. Throughout the years, Jaynie and Olivia had dance, art classes and piano, and James was part of an organization called the Knickerbocker Greys in New York City.

*Family portrait on Guard Hill Road; l-r: James,
Me, Jim, Olivia, Jaynie, Mother. 1955.*

*In front of Mother's house, Mayville; l-r Jaynie,
Olivia, James. 1956.*

Family resemblance. Clockwise from top: Jim in his 20's; Olivia around 12, James around 10.

I had to divide the children up in the schools they attended. Because Jaynie was born at the end of November, she was the youngest in her class when she started kindergarten and her teacher thought it best if she waited a year before going into 1st grade. With only fourteen months between her and Olivia, Olivia would have been in her class and the school didn't think this was a good idea. I sent Jaynie to the Bedford Rippowam School, a private, top-of-the-line school like Greenwich Country Day. We sent Olivia to Cisqua in the neighboring town of Mt. Kisco. Named after an Indian chief, it had been founded by a woman named Lady Gabriel who wanted French taught starting in Kindergarten. When James was ready to go to Kindergarten I had to choose which of the two schools to send him to, and decided on Cisqua since it was small and not as structured. Jaynie stayed on at Rippowam, which had a little more social standing because it had been there longer.

We had the usual menagerie, not only because of my love for animals, but because it teaches children—supposedly—responsibility and compassion. There was Pom Pom, a standard poodle and later Fifi, a miniature poodle. There was a Mexican burro, the kind with the cross on her back, named Cleo. She lived in a little horse barn at the bottom of our lawn until we put in the pool and made her house into a bath house. Every so often she got out and ran around outside trying to get into the house. I'm surprised we didn't let her in. There were rabbits, a large fish tank, South Carolina game cocks and a rooster. Then there was Vichyssoise, a white cat who met her demise by a car, and a calico stray who showed up and stayed. A stray German Shepherd mix dog we named Barron also just appeared, and

James and Pom Pom, circa 1961.

we took him in. When James was about twelve, we got him a

dog from the animal shelter that he named Pierre. One day Pierre got loose, and although we looked for him for days we never found him. James was heartbroken. People were supposed to be responsible and not let dogs run, but Pierre was fairly difficult to contain. The dogcatcher would pick up stray dogs, so perhaps that's what happened. Years later, James and Olivia gave me Genghis Khan who was part Poodle and part Yorkie. Fairly soon after that, I got Ollie Khan, who was a Lhasa Apso.

cs

Most summers I drove the children to Mayville to stay with my mother from around the 4th of July until Labor Day. I returned to Bedford, but went back to join them for several weeks in August, usually without my husband. The children loved to jump off the footbridge and swim in the Rock River; we often got huge inner tubes to float around in. We'd always drive "Up North" to Uncle Rude and Auntie Bernice's log cabin in Chetek—one of my children's favorite things to do. The cabin, nestled in tall Norwegian pines, sat on one of five connected lakes. Uncle Rude and Auntie Bernice had a special knack with the children, always making them feel totally at home and very special, providing fun and adventurous things for them to do. The endless candy, popcorn and huge bowls of ice cream every night contributed to the children's eagerness to visit.

Every spring vacation we'd go to Florida. I'd drive down with the children, and my husband would fly down. This was before Route 95 had been built, so we took Route 1 all the way down. They especially loved crossing the Chesapeake Bay Bridge, which was almost five miles long. Route 1 went through all these little towns, and they knew just which drive-ins to stop at for a great, thick milkshake. This was before McDonald's was everywhere, so the drive-ins had real personality. We spent two nights on Route 1; Whispering Pines was their favorite place. Once when my mother was visiting us she broke her arm, and realizing she couldn't do much in Mayville, decided to join us. I remember those drives down and back as being really fun and loved doing the trip with my children.

Yellowstone; l-r: Jaynie, Olivia, Me, James, 1965.

My children have always said that the summer we rented a camper tent and made a huge loop through the West for a month was the best vacation they had as children. Jaynie was thirteen, Olivia twelve, and James was about ten.

The year before at the Dodge County Fair, I had seen those campers that you hitched to your car; when you got to your destination you'd pop the tent up. I thought it would be fun to camp, although I had never in my life camped before. We were a little ahead of the camping rage; people weren't doing it much in those days, so it was just beginning to become popular.

I drove our big Oldsmobile station wagon out to Mayville with the children and rented a camper near the Horicon Marsh, over in Waupun. Jim was going to fly out and meet us in Mayville, but he was delayed for business reasons so the children and I started out. Jim would meet us in a few days in the Black Hills of South Dakota. We left at four o'clock in the morning, my mother anxiously waving us off.

We had a reservation in a campground in Iowa where we would camp that first night. Just over the Mississippi into Iowa, all of a sudden we felt this jolt and the children looked out the back. There was the camper barreling down the road behind us—unattached. Fortunately, we were on a detour and it was basically a straight road. Behind the loose camper I could see a few cars, including a pickup truck. Not knowing what else to do, I slowed down and let the camper crash into the back of the car, making a dent. The children thought it was a riot, but I wasn't so entertained, imagining what could have happened if we had been going fast on the highway.

The kind man in the truck had a trailer hitch, so he attached our wayward trailer to the back of his truck and we followed him to the next town where there happened to be a welding shop. At the shop, they dropped everything they were doing to fix the hitch for us, so we were able to get to the campground in time.

Earlier that day a tornado had whipped through the campground leaving trees strewn all over the place. We had the last campsite at the end with nothing but cornfields as far as we could see, and a strong wind blowing incessantly. We got in the camper that had legs supposedly to hold it firm, but it didn't feel very secure to me. I was sure the wind was going to blow us over, but somehow we made it through the night upright. We had a Coleman stove which I didn't have the slightest idea how to light but luckily James and Olivia, who were always very good at those things, were able to figure it out.

I didn't have the slightest idea how to back the trailer up, so when we needed gas I had to make sure I pulled into a station that I could pull straight ahead to exit. When we got into a campground, we'd pull up, unhitch the trailer, and all four of us would back it in by hand.

In the prairie town of Wall on the edge of the South Dakota Badlands, we stopped at the famous Wall's Drug Store. It had a small pharmacy to earn its name, but then all these connected buildings and amusements. I have some pictures of the children looking out of those cutout heads that made them seem as if they were sitting on bucking broncos.

On to Mt. Rushmore to see the famous monument of the presidents carved into the rockface. When we got to the Black Hills, we found a campsite right by a beautiful little lake called Sylvan Lake. Jim couldn't get out for another four days, so I was there alone with the children, hearing tornado warnings every day. It poured rain but it didn't stop us from doing things.

We finally picked Jim up in Rapid City, South Dakota. He wanted to make sure the hitch was really secure, so we had it double-checked and fixed more permanently. Then we headed down through Nebraska and over into Colorado where we stopped in Cripple Creek, an old gold mining town. Cripple Creek is known as a place where many artists and writers go; now it's become kind of artsy. Even back in the 1960s they had a really good summer theater that was quite well known, and we saw one of those old fashioned melodramas, which was fun. We headed west to Mesa Verde, the amazing Pueblo Indian cliff dwellings where you had to go through narrow cracks and climb a wooden ladder. Now you can't go through them anymore because it's considered too much of an insurance risk, plus they don't want the cliffs to get damaged. From there, we went to the North Rim of the Grand Canyon, then up to Bryce Canyon in Utah, which is an unbelievably beautiful state.

We had planned to stop every couple of nights in a motel, but we ended up staying in a motel only twice on the whole trip. We were having such a great time camping, and made sure we stopped in campgrounds that had showers.

While we were on the road, we had things like peanut butter which we kept in an ice storage chest, so when everybody got hungry one of the children would crawl to the back of the station wagon and make sandwiches for everyone while we kept driving.

From Utah we shot up to the northwestern corner of Wyoming to Yellowstone National Park and the Grand Tetons where we camped at Jenny Lake, one of the most beautiful mountain lakes in the country. It was the 4th of July and we left our big metal ice chest, the kind with latches, by the camper when we went away for the day. When we came back, a lot of people were standing around it. Apparently, a bear had tried to break into the chest and had made a major dent in it.

Exhilarated from our big adventure, the children and I drove back to Mayville, having covered eight states and thousands of miles. Jim had to get back to his job, so flew back.

 C3

The private schools around Bedford only went through 9th grade for girls and 8th for boys. After 9th grade,

Jaynie

Jaynie and Olivia went on to Rosemary Hall in Greenwich. In those days, it was considered educational to send your children to a Swiss school for a year to introduce them to Europe, so we decided that the girls would go to La Comb in the town of Rolle near Lausanne for their junior year. They'd return to Rosemary for their senior year. La Comb was a small school run by a couple and took only fifty girls from an international clientele. Along with academics and languages, there was an emphasis on sailing and skiing.

Jaynie was a good student and a talented artist. She also had a beautiful singing voice, which we didn't know about until we heard her sing a Christmas solo at St. Matthews Church when she was about twelve.

Between the ages of eight and ten, James belonged to the Knicker-bocker Greys, a very old organization founded in 1881 as an after school activity for boys before they went off to boarding school. Its purpose was to give cadets experiences that built character, leadership qualities, self esteem, social skills, empathy, public speaking, problem solving and perse-verance. It was very difficult to get into; you had to have many letters of reference. Every Saturday, James took the train

Olivia

into New York City and from Grand Central got on a bus to the 67th Street Armory on Park Avenue. We sent him there partly because we thought it was good training for him, but it was also the beginning of a young man's social life in New York—the precursor to attending all the debutante balls as an escort. Every spring, guests of honor such as Lucas Clay or Curtis Lamay, generals in the Army Air Force, came to the Knickerbocker Grays' spring review.

James

James went to boarding school at Brooks in Andover, Massachusetts in 8th grade. It was just something that you expected to do in those days—somewhat like the English sys-tem—and assured a better education, but it was very difficult to leave him there when we drove him up to school.

I think it would be interesting to know my children's real feelings about going away to school. That's just what was done in those days.

*Me, poolside, Guard Hill
Road. Late '60s.*

Back yard of Guard Hill Road house. Jaynie's graduation from Rippowam;
l-r: Me, Olivia, Jim, Jaynie, James, our pet rooster. 1968.

Virginia Wright and me (right). Daughters of the American Revolution Memorial Day Parade, Chappaqua, NY, 1980s.

ଓ 16 ଅ

Overt Activities of a Suburban Housewife

While I was raising our children, I wanted to have some out-of-the-home activities to balance my life as a wife and mother. I was invited to join the Junior League as a volunteer. To become a member, I had to take a provisional course, which entailed learning all the things the organization did.

With the group of Junior League volunteers, I toured the women's state prison, which was only about seven miles out of Bedford. The Bedford Hills Correctional Facility had many unwed mothers from New York City and people locked up for drug dealing. Many years later in the '80s, Jean Harris, the Smith College-educated head of a school and mistress of the Scarsdale Diet doctor, was incarcerated there after she shot her lover four times point blank in a fit of jealousy. Surrounding the prison was some of the most expensive real estate in Bedford. Years later when I became a real estate broker, if people mentioned it when I was showing them around, I'd say casually, "Oh, nobody in Bedford ever thinks about it; we just drive by."

We also visited a school for retarded children. Back then schools didn't mainstream children who were disabled; instead they put them in special schools, and members of the Junior League did a lot of volunteer teaching.

Once I became a full-fledged member of the Junior League, I could choose to volunteer in whatever interested me. The Junior League had parties and social events to raise the much-needed money for all these programs, and I became the Ways and Means Chairman and Chairman of the Dance, in charge of all fundraisers. The big fundraiser was the yearly ball, and one year I organized the entire event.

Jim and I went to St. Matthew's Church, a beautiful old church built in the early 1800s with a double aisle, pew boxes with the little latches, and prayer cushions done in needlepoint by ladies of the church. Before the church was built, when there was a parish, John Jay—a Founding Father, Chief Justice of the United States, and Governor of New York—was one of its original vestrymen. I was active in the church and taught 4th grade Sunday School for several years while my children attended. Every Christmas the church had a huge fair and I was in charge of the "gourmet table." No "bake sale" for Bedford! Church members cooked quite elegant things, and people reserved cakes or pies way in advance. It was a big fundraiser and St. Matthews, being very well off, was one of the few churches that was able to give money to other churches that needed it.

I decided to become a member of the Daughters of the American Revolution, not only because I'm very interested in American history, but also because I was proud of the fact that a member of my family, Nathan Blodgett was in the Revolutionary War. An avid history buff, I loved the idea of continuity from one generation to another through history. I think it's fun to find out who your ancestors were, what they were like, and what they did. People forget so fast and it seems most people today can't even name their great grand-parents. Often children don't really know what their grand-parents were like, or how they were affected by the times in which they grew up. That's one of the reasons why my children asked me to do this personal history.

To become a member of the DAR you needed to prove you had a relative who helped the revolutionary cause in some way, by either fighting or supplying food, shelter, any-thing; you did not have to be a soldier. I had to go back and do lots of research to verify my claim that Nathan Blodgett was an active member of the Constitutional Army in Connecticut. I got a registered DAR number, so my daughters could automatically become members.

Many people assume African Americans aren't eligible to be in the DAR, but that's absolutely not true. As long as a person can prove he or she helped in some way, it doesn't matter what race they are; in fact, there were a couple of quite famous black people who helped in the Revolutionary War. They were probably slaves, but they still fought, or might have helped in another way.

Before the Kennedy Center was built in Washington, the DAR owned the largest meeting place owned by women in all of DC, Constitution Hall, which was built in 1929 and was quite impressive. Big concerts and anything major were held there when space was needed.

Since 1936, many people have thought negatively about the DAR for what they think was the organization's re-fusal to let Marian Anderson perform. Washington, DC at that time was a segregated city, and the DAR was complying with the local law when they adopted a rule excluding Afri-can Americans from performing in Constitution Hall. In 1936, Marian Anderson's manager Sol Hurok attempted to book her there, but was refused based on the "white per-formers only policy." The DAR got plenty of bad publicity and there was some question whether the DAR could have overridden the local law and made an exception. Marian An-derson did not appear at Constitution Hall, but was invited by Eleanor Roosevelt to appear instead on the steps of the Lincoln Memorial. Mrs. Roosevelt had such enormous popularity and entrée to all the news media, which created all the feeling surrounding this unfortunate event.

Very few people know that the DAR does much to support poor people in Appalachia and has several colleges and boarding schools for the mountain people. They support some schools in the poor parts of North and South Carolina where there are descendants of early Scottish and Irish immigrants. In the 1930s and 1940s, several boarding schools were run entirely by funds from the DAR for families deep in the mountains whose children couldn't get to school on a daily basis. The DAR also does historical restoration of cemeteries and gravestones to keep American history alive.

After the assassination of Martin Luther King in 1968, riots broke out in Washington, DC. The city was in shambles, but the DAR was one of the first groups to return to DC to stay in hotels near the White House after the riots calmed down. I was part of a group that went to stay in those hotels, which had lost lots of business due to the riots. The hotels were very appreciative of our stance and highly complimentary as well.

I was active in the DAR, attending monthly meetings. I was Regent of the chapter for four years and National Defense Chairman for twenty years. Most years I joined several thousand other women from all over the United States at the Constitutional Convention in Washington, DC in April during cherry blossom time.

Back in the '50s we went into New York for the huge parade down Fifth Avenue when General MacArthur returned from the Korean War. He had been fired by Truman, and when he returned there was a huge protest because so many people really loved Douglas MacArthur. My son James has a book signed by him that my husband bought. When MacArthur died, his body lying in the 67th Street Armory, I went into New York City and stood in line one whole afternoon to pay my respects. He was considered a great hero by most people.

In the mid-50s, Jim and I helped organize the New York State Conservative Party in an attempt to bring the Republican Party further to the right. Nelson Rockefeller and the heads of the Republican Party were much too liberal for what we were looking for; they were becoming more and more big government and proponents of more taxes. I was also running on the ticket for the State Constitutional Convention for the Conservative Party.

Back in the '60s I campaigned to repeal the income tax and to make the Post Office private. It had never occurred to me that it should be anything other than run by the government until I looked into it. I discovered that it could be much better run, and probably be making money, if it weren't overloaded with bureaucracy and with employees getting retirement benefits forever. I remember Mayville had a Post Office when I was very young that was in a store and wasn't much bigger than a room. Today's Post Office in Mayville was built in 1932 by the WPA to make work for people in the middle of the Depression. It's beautiful, but one of the largest public buildings in town.

I also became a member of the John Birch Society, which started around 1958 and in the beginning got very bad press. *Life Magazine* had a critical, six-page article about the John Birch Society; after I read the article I thought, *Boy, that's something that I want to join!* When *Life Magazine* was against something, it usually made me the opposite. The slogan of the John Birch society is "less government, more individual responsibility, with God's help a better world." They believed that all these things weren't just happening by accident; that there were people in the government with Socialist leanings and that there was a lot of pro-Communist literature in government.

One of things the John Birch Society did in the early 1960s was to have "Card Parties." They made these little cards the size of calling cards that said *buy your communist merchandise at ...* and then the name of the store. At the time, there was very strong feeling against trading with communist countries. Volunteers would go to the stores and put the cards into coat pockets or under the covers of pots and pans, etc. When people got their purchases home, they'd find the card, then call the department store, upset. The John Birch Society had started this on the west coast and it was really quite effective, so we tried it in White Plains. I decided to volunteer, and about fifty of us went to Klein's Department Store. We were supposed to be careful, just slip a card in, not open anything sealed, not let anyone see us, then quietly leave. But stores were on to it by then. Seven of us, including one innocent man who was just shopping for a Christmas present for his wife, were arrested by the store police and taken to the security office. I was wearing a fur coat and they said over the loudspeaker, "We got one in a fur coat."

We were held in the security office by plain clothes guards for four hours without being able to make a phone call. The leader of our group got into a fight with a security officer right there in the office. It was getting dark, and finally the police arrived and hustled us all into a paddy wagon. Halfway through the trip to the police station, the driver stopped at a phone booth so we could make calls and then took us to police station where we had to post bail. In those days you didn't carry an extra $50 around, nor were there cash machines. My husband had to call our attorney and drive into the city to bail me out. Fortunately he had $50 in the house.

The case of the "Innocent Seven," as we were called, was taken to court, so we had to hire an attorney. It was amazing to me how the store detectives got up and lied under oath. They said we were trying to create a riot in the store, that several people took women's lingerie and stamped on it. That was totally untrue; we did just the opposite, trying to be anonymous. Klein's dropped the case with us signing a waiver of $1 apiece. We probably should have turned around and sued the store for false arrest, but I think everybody was glad the case was dropped.

In 1960, Barry Goldwater published his book *Conscience of a Conservative,* which impressed me because his ideas meshed with mine: the basic philosophy of less government, more individual responsibility. The smaller the government, the better I like it, and more participation on the local level is best of all. When people can vote to take from some to give to others it's Socialism, which I'm against. I'm very much against socialized medicine; it certainly hasn't worked anywhere. Case in point—many people come from Canada for medical care here.

I was president of the Bedford Republican Club for a while in the '60s. About a year before Goldwater announced his campaign for the presidency against Lyndon Johnson, we started a Goldwater headquarters in Bedford, the first in New York. A group of us, including my husband and my mother, went up to New Hampshire to help get him in the primary election there. Some of us Goldwater backers started Freedom Presentations where we had monthly speakers who spoke on different topics such as repealing the income tax and various subjects that were strongly anti-Communist.

Early 1950s. Photo by Hal Phyfe

❧ 17 ❧
The Troops Return

*O*ver the years I lived in Bedford, the men I had been very involved with before I married resurfaced in one way or another.

Eric

When I was on my honeymoon I heard that Eric had married. Somehow he knew I had married, although I hadn't told him. He and his wife had one child.

Jim and I went to California to attend a business convention shortly after returning to New York and visited Eric and his wife in Newport Beach. Although it was very difficult for me to see Eric, I felt it was the right thing to do, not only because of my long connection with him, but also with his parents.

Eric visited us in Bedford when I was pregnant with either Olivia or James. He and my husband got along well, so it was a good visit and he even spent the night. I never told Jim how I felt about Eric, but when he visited that time, I felt the same way about him that I always had.

One time Eric and his wife came through New York on their way back from Sweden. Jim's company carried some of the insurance at the United Nations, so I took them on a private tour of the UN and we had lunch in the delegates' dining room.

Eric died very young in the late 1960s when he and his wife were in Sweden. His mother sent me a telegram to let me know, and we sent flowers. I remember going shopping in New York City the day I heard of his death and crying most of the day.

Jack

In 1953, James and I were invited to Jack Kennedy's wedding. It was a rather small wedding, held in the picturesque St. Mary's Roman Catholic Church in Newport, Rhode Island, but over eight hundred guests attended the reception at the farm owned by Mr. Auchincloss, Jackie's stepfather. Langdon and Gloria were there, and practically every senator who was important. My husband knew Jackie's mother, Janet Lee, from his bachelor days in New York when he was eighteen or nineteen. I can't say I felt any great emotion seeing Jack get married. When I was going through the reception line, the person managing it said I was holding up the line because Jack and I were talking a little longer than most people. I felt like saying, *hey, we were lovers once; we have a lot to talk about!* Of course I didn't!

David

I was just going along, raising my children, being an innocent suburban housewife when I got a call in 1954 from the House Committee on Un-American Activities regarding David Schine. Gloria had told them to call me because they wanted to find out all they could about David from people who knew him.

In the early '50s, Senator Joseph McCarthy had made claims that Communists had infiltrated the government, and he verbally attacked many politicians and non-governmental

170

people. He maintained that the government was neglecting to deal with these Communist infiltrators. David had been brought on staff by his friend Roy Cohn, who had become Senator McCarthy's chief lawyer, and Roy and David went on a tour of Europe to scrutinize United States Information Agency libraries for pro-Communist literature. Here were these young kids going around making a big fuss in the Army libraries in Europe. I felt David was right to be investigating, but knowing David, I suspect he didn't go about it the right way. He could be very officious about things.

Later that year David was conscripted into the Army. The hearings claimed that Roy began asking military officials to give David a commission, pressuring them not to send him overseas, to give him more leave than usual and light duties.

In 1954 the Army-McCarthy hearings were held. The Army accused McCarthy and Roy Cohn of using pressure on the Army for preferential treatment of David, and McCarthy and Cohn accused the Army of using the issue to squash McCarthy's investigations into Communist infiltration of the Army. I didn't have any information about any kind of political issue that would have made a difference, so I was never required to appear at the hearings. I did watch the hearings every day, however, obviously very interested because David was one of the major players in the proceedings.

I knew David was manipulative and would have pulled rank. They used him as the touch point for these hearings, but there was really another agenda behind all of that, I think. At the beginning I was on the side against McCarthy, and knew that David would have used his influence to get leave from the Army base but later on, long after the hearings were over, I changed my viewpoint to feeling McCarthy was right.

Interestingly, many years later David met Olivia in a venture capital meeting. Olivia was working at an investment bank and her venture capitalist associates asked her to sit in and listen to a business plan of which David Schine was one of the promoters. Olivia recalled the name and asked him if he knew her mother. He said he did, and said to say hello.

David died along with his wife and one of his twin sons in a plane crash in 1996. The single engine plane, piloted by his son, went down shortly after takeoff from Burbank Airport.

Jack Again

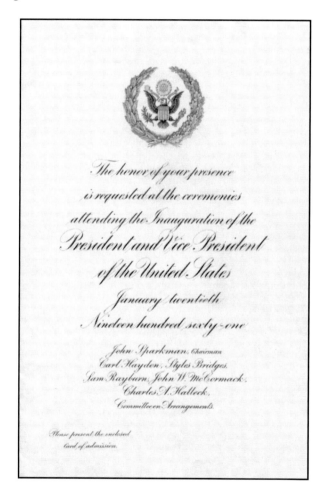

In 1961, Jim and I were invited to John Kennedy's inauguration. Of course, I've saved the program and tickets.

We stayed outside Washington DC with Francie Stone's mother, who was about eighty-five years old and one of the "cave dwellers," as old Washingtonians were known. John Sherman Cooper, a well-known senator from Kentucky, lived across the street from her, and on the day of the inauguration when a big snowstorm threatened to practically close Washington down, Senator Cooper offered to drive us into town in his limousine since he could easily get through all the barricades and events that were going on prior to the ceremony. We went to his office in the Senate and rode the little train that went between the Senate and the House of Representatives before going to the inaugural ceremonies.

Glancing through the audience, I could see many well-known people: Senator Keating and Senator Javitz from New York, McClellan, Symington, Pat Muntz, the entire Kennedy family, the Truman family, Senator Hallock, Ted Sorenson, Kenneth Galbraith, Peter Schlesinger, Peter Lawford, the Frelinghuysens, and Chicago's Mayor Daley. Our reserved seats were on an open terrace, allowing us to look down and see the speaker.

Robert Frost had written a poem called "Dedication" specially for the occasion. Not only did the podium catch on fire due to faulty electrical wiring (we could see smoke coming out), but when he started to read the poem he couldn't see the words because the sun had come out and the glare reflecting off the snow was shining into his eyes. He stumbled a bit and gave up, instead reciting from memory in his beautifully commanding voice, "The Gift Outright."

While Jack was making his inaugural speech, it was so cold we decided we'd go back in the Capitol, which at that time wasn't so restricted; you could walk around, go in and out, unlike now when there are so many guards. There was nobody in the hallways except Joe Martin, Speaker of the House. We said hello and walked down the hallway with him.

After Jack finished his speech, he came back into the Rotunda of the Capitol. We were standing right there, so I was one of the first people to shake hands with him right after he had been sworn in. Jim tried to take a picture, but the

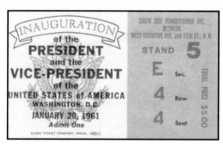

Secret Service practically knocked the camera out of his hand, probably thinking there might be a bomb in the camera.

Our seats were in a reserved section along the parade route, but halfway through the parade it was getting very cold, so we went on to a party Langdon Marvin was hosting at the Hay Adams, also on the parade route. There were many people there who had

opted to watch the parade from the comfort of Langdon's suite, drinking cocktails, rather than brave the chill of January in Washington, DC.

I was talking with various people and asked one man what he did for a living. He said he was a writer and his book was being made into a movie. Suddenly I put two and two together and realized I was talking to John Steinbeck. When the party was over and everybody left to get dressed for the balls, we just happened to stand next to the Steinbecks waiting for taxis and visited with them again for quite a while.

We went to the ball at the National Armory. I wore that black velvet designer dress, the famous dress, which was the kind of ball gown I could wear even now.

After we got back to Bedford, Langdon wrote us a note saying:

I'm so glad that you and Jayne came to the inaugu-
ration. On Sunday afternoon there came an opportunity to
see JFK but you had already
gone back, so I rounded up the
remaining members of our
group and had a cheerful word
with him at the White House. I
am sending you separately a
memento of the inauguration,
Cordially, Langdon.

Langdon had tried to get in touch with us before we left, but unfortunately we drove back early. It would have been a great party because we would have been in the private family quarters of the White House and seen Jack afterward.

og

A few years later, Jim and I were going down to Washington to a conservative political action event called Human Events Conference sponsored by *The Chicago Tribune.* I wrote to Ted Reardon who was Jack's personal organizer to ask if we could have a tour of the White House while we were down there. I knew I could write my senator to request this, but I wrote directly to Ted. He wrote back saying he'd be glad to arrange a special White House tour, and that we should just call when we got down to Washington. We got on a tour of about twenty people quite early in the morning and saw a lot of the White House. When the tour was finished the guide said, "Is Jayne Blodgett Murray in this group?" I said yes, and he told me to call this number on the White House phone. I got Ted Reardon who said if we'd like to wait a little we could see the president.

We sat in the pressroom for awhile and then went into the Oval Office. There was nobody there, and it was like being in a small town office—just amazing—very quiet with nobody around. We walked around and could have picked up anything. Then Jack walked in. I shook hands with him and said, "Hello, Jack, or should I call you Mr. President?"

It was nice that he asked to see us. I'm sure he was curious about what my husband was like. We sat down and visited with him; he was very outgoing, asking about our children, and I asked him about his family. He wanted to know why we were in Washington. I didn't want to tell him it was for the Human Events Conference because it was considered right-wing, so I just said, "Oh we're down here for a conference, but we're members of the loyal opposition."

A couple of months after that he was assassinated. I was at the hairdresser's when I heard the news and it was a shock, but I don't remember feeling as if I was going to go into mourning over it. I remember I had a bumper sticker on the back of my car that said *Kennedy for King, Goldwater for President,* and after he was shot somebody saw the bumper sticker and banged on the back of my car making a fist at me. Emotions were, of course, running high and I took the bumper sticker off.

Harold

In the late '60s, Harold's father was shot and killed. I heard it on the car radio. He was driving home to Brooklyn late at night and someone rammed into the back of his car on purpose at a stoplight. They saw 'MD' on his license plate, figured he'd have drugs, and when he got out to check the damage, they shot him point blank. I don't think they ever caught the murderer. Apparently license plates don't say 'MD' anymore due to drug related holdups.

I wrote Harold a letter to tell him how sorry I was about his father, and found out he was living in Fairfield, which is about thirty miles from Bedford. Shortly after I received a letter back from him, we met for lunch. I hadn't seen him eighteen years. I had liked him before when I was seeing him in New York, but I wasn't really in love with him and was under so much pressure to marry him. Jim's and my relationship had been strained for some time now, our differences more pronounced than our common ground. It was clear we were heading for divorce. Harold and I started seeing each other again, although we were both married.

During the year Jaynie and Olivia were at La Comb, I made a plan to go visit them and arranged with Harold to meet me in Switzerland, but he didn't. He lied to me, telling me his wife was being operated on and he couldn't come. I realized that he never really had the nerve to go ahead and do anything.

That became a rather bleak time for me. Harold wasn't calling me; in fact, he was actually trying to stop seeing me. He wouldn't get divorced and I *was* getting divorced. I had thought he was going to get divorced and marry me.

Gloria knew the agony I was in and gave me a little leather book, kind of a diary with dates. She wrote notes on the days saying things like "clean your drawers," "call Bootsie," "color your hair," or "do exercises"—things to ground me and give me structure. It was her way of helping me believe I was going to be all right, to stay hopeful. I was supposed to read these each day and then write my own thoughts to make me feel better. She also told me to ...*describe the pain and loneliness; write down when it's worse, be as scientific as possible,* wisely knowing I had to admit those negative feelings before I could move on.

I wrote: "...one would feel as though one would like to crawl into a dark hole and just hide...." Super dramatic, but this was what I was feeling at the time.

Harold and I stopped seeing each other, but we always kept in touch and continued to talk on the phone even until a couple of months ago.

*Ollie Khan and me in the house I built on
Guard Hill Road, early 1980s.*

❧ 18 ❧

Lettin' Go and Movin' On

When I first started seeing Harold, I wasn't conscious of being depressed, but at some point I realized my depression had been subtly festering over the past few years. When the girls went away to Switzerland for a year James was still at home, but the next year he went to boarding school and the girls would be graduating the following year. I was beginning to get a taste of the typical empty nest syndrome that many women get in their forties. I also was beginning to admit that I was unhappy in my marriage. I saw Harold for about a year before Jim and I divorced in 1973; looking back, reconnecting with Harold was the precipitating event for Jim's and my split up.

During this time I met Zel Heinneman who became my closest friend in later life, as Gloria had been in my earlier years. Jim and I had met Zel and her husband Ed at a party in a beautiful townhouse in New York. It was black tie, and Zel was incredibly glamorous in her formal evening gown. We started talking and immediately became friendly. She was just my age, an actress, very outgoing, had a terrific personality, and always had a circle of men around her. She could tell great stories and jokes which I thought was a great talent. Several days later, I met Zel for lunch in New York. Zel and Ed, a very well-known aircraft designer of fighter planes during World War II, lived in Westport, Connecticut. Jim and I were still married, so we saw each other regularly as two couples. After I got divorced and was going through so much emotional turmoil, Zel was very sympathetic. I'd go up to her house in Westport, and we often went shopping or out to lunch together. We remained very good friends until a couple of years ago when she went into a retirement home in California. Her daughter Vicky was a little older than my daughters, very bright, and went to Harvard to study law.

Jim and I shared the house on Guard Hill Road for about a year until our divorce was final, and then we sold it. My attorney said I would be much better taking a lump sum of money rather than just getting a set amount per month because I never knew my husband's income—a Victorian concept! I had no idea whether he had plenty of money or not, and I didn't own part of the house.

I remember clearly the day Jim and I met for lunch to sign the divorce papers, and it was definitely sad. You don't have children and spend twenty years with a man and not feel a certain deep connection. He rented a place in Bedford for a while and then moved back into the city.

ର

After high school Jaynie went to Finch College in New York for a year but chose not to finish. Instead, she went to Italy with a singing group that sang all over the country. When she returned to the US, she worked in a shop and did some acting—notably the lead in *Hedda Gabler* in Stockbridge. There she met Spencer Keyes, who was from Washington, DC, and had Elizabeth in 1977.

Jaynie and Elizabeth lived with me some of the time. That was when I was buying houses, renovating them and then selling them as a broker with Ginnel Real Estate. When it was time to put one on the market, I always moved some furniture and plants in, and often Jaynie and Elizabeth stayed there, keeping the house occupied and ready to show at all times. It made the house more homey and helped people envision living there.

Olivia graduated from Stanford and then went to work in New York in the financial industry before returning to Stanford to earn a Masters degree in business. She later returned to New York and continued to work in corporate finance. She was married and divorced. While married, she and her husband bought the parlor floor of a beautiful old Brooklyn Heights Brownstone just off the Promenade. Olivia later moved back to Manhattan nearer her office and nearer where Jim lived, so she was able to assist him.

James went to the University of Pennsylvania where he got a degree in Business. There he met Susie Hinkle who had grown up practically next door in New Canaan, but they had never met until they had a class together his first year. They were married in 1979. He got a job at Chase Manhattan Bank and they lived in Brooklyn Heights for a year before Chase sent him abroad. For the next twenty-nine years they lived in Paris, Hong Kong, London and Sin-

Me, James and Susie; Ollie and Ghengis Khan.

gapore, during which time they had their three beautiful daughters—Sarah, Emily and Abigail.

❧

I bought a couple of acres of the Guard Hill Road property from my husband when we divorced, planning to build a house there. In the meantime, I rented a small house, built before 1700, down a little dirt road named Clinton Road. I would have liked to buy it, but it belonged to the estate of a family who didn't want to sell it. It was just my kind of place—old and charming, with a fireplace not only in the living room, but also a small one up in the bedroom and those great Colonial low ceilings and wide floorboards. I lived there two or three years and then built the house on Guard Hill Road, just around the corner. I was there for the rest of the time I was living in Bedford.

I built the house around a door I had bought at a wonderful place in Stamford called United Housewrecking, which specialized in salvaging furniture and architectural elements from houses being demolished. It was a beautiful antique interior door saved from the Hudson River mansion belonging to the former governor of New York, Herbert Lehman, but it was so thick and heavy that I used it for my front entrance.

Bill and Margaret in front of the house I built.

I built the house on top of a hill where the land sloped gently down and flattened into an area which I dredged because it was so swampy. I also had a pond dug. I wasn't sure if it was going to fill up or not, but it did, and we were able to swim in it.

I always loved a lot of light and the feeling of inside being open to the outside, so the house had skylights, decks, balconies, French doors and casement windows made extra long because I love windows that almost touch the floor. A window seat looked out to the hot tub and the pond. I put in beautiful wide floorboards, which people always thought were antique pine. The kitchen was small, but had a really great stove and a direct view into the dining room and living room. James built wonderful bookshelves in the living room. What I really loved was using the frame from the antique door to make the fireplace mantle, covering some of the molding with shelving paper that looked just like marble. The house, semi-contemporary but filled with old touches, was airy, comfortable and, I thought, very atmospheric.

Later, I built a garage with a little apartment over it that I rented to Henry Williams, a long time friend. It provided a helpful income. Henry's wife had died, and he wanted to marry me, but by then I was going with Charlie. Henry was a sweet man, I liked him as a friend, but I didn't want to marry him. In the afternoon he'd come over with a tray, calling "teatime" and we'd sit on the deck right off the living room and sip tea. He was Welsh and felt it was very English. Even when he had to move into a nursing home, he had his teapot and made himself tea every afternoon. Henry loved cats and dogs and had a pug when he lived above the garage. At his previous home there were feral cats around; he didn't mind chloroforming the kittens they produced, which I thought was awful. I know he felt just terrible when he ran over my little Lhasa Apso, Ollie Khan by accident right in my driveway. He came up to the door with my dog in his arms and tears in his eyes.

Henry and I talked often on the phone until he died in 2009. I received a lovely note from his son:

Dad died last night at 3 am from pneumonia. He lived a long life made easier by your friendship in his later

*years. Thanks for being there for him when he needed
someone to play with. Hope all's well in Wisconsin.*
    All the best. Martyn

After my divorce, I had to do something to earn some
money. I hadn't really thought about it at the time, and I'm
wondering now how I ever had the nerve to get divorced not
knowing what I was going to live on. It seemed that real estate was the easiest thing for me to do, and I kind of fell into
it. Before I got a broker's license, I started working for a man
who was the head of the Republican Club in Mt. Kisco, whom
I knew through my political activities. He had a small real
estate office, and I worked for him less than a year, although
I really didn't like the way he was running the office. There
were three or four girls in the office, and he didn't want any
of us to wear pants. One week when he was away, at my in-
stigation we all rebelled and wore slacks. He heard about it
when he got back and was angry. I told him his rule was im-
practical and didn't make any sense since we we're constantly walking up stairs and sometimes even climbing lad-
ders. It didn't change his mind at all.

Luckily, I met Helen Ginnel. She was another older
woman in my life like Francie Stone had been—a lot of fun,
very kind, and kind of a mentor to me. Helen hired me partly
because I had been living in Bedford long enough to know
many people, which is always a plus in real estate.

Helen was from Scarsdale and had a real estate business. She bred Labrador Retrievers and also owned a couple
of horses she loved to ride. She was different from many
people I knew, very laid back, always had a cigarette between
her fingers, and liked to sit with her feet up on the desk. Very
interested in houses, she had a good head about them and
was very helpful to me not only in real estate deals, but also
advising me when I wanted to buy a house. Helen and I were
also friendly on a social basis, so often I went to her house
for dinner and occasionally got to ride on their boat. I really
enjoyed working for Helen.

I sold real estate for a long time—from my divorce until I moved to Narrowsburg, New York in 1993; even then I kept my license. I was the top producer several times but left real estate, partly because computers came in and things were getting very automated. I also didn't want to be the oldest person in the office, with people thinking they were going to have to drag me around to open houses. There had been one agent named Janet Armor, who was a little five-foot tall woman, fun, and sort of the elder stateswoman in our office. She was a good friend of William Randolph Hearst, Jr., whom I saw regularly at her dinner and cocktail parties. Towards the end of her tenure, she used to drive up to the office and almost run into the fence in front. One time when she didn't come into the office within a reasonable amount of time, we went out and found her asleep in the car. I didn't want that to happen to me.

Guard Hill Road. Back row, l-r: James, Me, Olivia, Larry Marks, Jaynie; front row: Susie, Elizabeth. Early '80s.

Charlie and me, late 1970s

ᑫ 19 ᑭ

Just When You Think You'll
Never Love Again...

S ometimes I think Charlie might not have died if we'd
  gotten married and he'd taken better care of himself. I
  have a feeling that if he and I hadn't broken up he
might not have had the stroke, and we could have been together much longer.

I met Charlie LeBoutillier Homer through his niece,
Gail Sneed, Helen's executive secretary. Gail lived in an old
Colonial up in South Salem. She had good taste and many
lovely antiques. She was a very social person with a great
sense of humor, and I liked her very much. When she said
her uncle was coming for the weekend and she'd like to have
me come up for dinner to meet him, I was happy to accept
her invitation. Jaynie and Elizabeth, who was only three
months old, were living with me at the time, so they both
joined me.

When I first met Charlie I wasn't particularly drawn to
him. That evening he said he'd like to see me again soon. A
month or two later, when I was going to James' graduation
from the University of Pennsylvania, Charlie and I made

plans to get together since he lived in Philadelphia. We met at James' fraternity house and Charlie decided everybody—James, Susie, their friend Alan and I—should all come back to his place for dinner rather than going out. He said he had plenty of food. We all drove out to Charlie's place in Gladwyn on Philadelphia's "Main Line," named because it was originally on the railroad's main line.

His home was a lovely rambling stone house set back from the road, and he was living there basically as a bachelor because his wife was in an institution. She had been a United States champion women's squash player and a good golfer, but also a serious alcoholic. I went into the kitchen with Charlie, and he opened the refrigerator revealing a whole stack of frozen dinners, his idea of plenty of food for dinner. His kitchen was surprisingly well-equipped and the rest of the house was beautifully decorated. It turned out that Charlie was quite a perfectionist and loved beautiful things like the old Windsor chairs around his dining room table, and lovely blue and white Staffordshire china that many people collect. I liked that about him. We had a fun dinner, all played some bridge, and then James, Susie and Alan went back to the university. I stayed at Charlie's, and I remember putting a chair behind my door when I went to bed, not sure what Charlie might have in mind.

This second time I saw him I thought he was very nice. He was close to twenty years older, which fit my "preferred man profile." Although he was very serious and quite proper, he was also lots of fun. Maybe the best way to describe him is kind of cuddly. He drank a little too much but, thankfully, not so much that he got obnoxious. He belonged to the Marion Cricket Club, a very old club in Main Line Philadelphia and often took me there.

The next day Gail's mother—Charlie's sister—who lived in Pound Ridge, was down in Philadelphia for some reason and we had lunch. She told me Charlie really liked me. When I got back to Bedford, Charlie called and I remember talking on the kitchen phone when he said, "I think I'm falling in love with you."

From then on, whenever he came up to Bedford I'd see him. His daughter Anne and his two grandsons lived right nearby in Bedford Village, so he'd come up for weekends and stay with me. His other daughter Bicky (short for Elizabeth) was an excellent artist and lived in Boston where we once went to her house for dinner. Although I was very friendly with his daughters, his son Charles, Jr. for some reason didn't seem to like me. He had a house near his father's and had never married.

Charlie's family was originally from the Isle of Man in the English Channel, but Charlie had grown up in Chestnut Hill outside of Philadelphia. His father made lots of money in the 1920s, but lost it in the Depression, so they moved up to Connecticut where he became a yacht broker. Charlie was a promising football player in high school with ambitions of going to Princeton and playing football. His uncle, Supreme Court Justice Homer, had money and was going to pay for Charlie to go there. I'm not sure if his father had died at that point, but Charlie never went to college because Uncle Homer thought Charlie should first work in the steel rolling mills. He worked really hard until he was twenty and then created his own company, National Steel, which was a small company, not like US Steel. During World War II, he enlisted and became a Naval officer in charge of commandeering allocations of copper—something to do with the Army or Navy and the whole War Department rationing things.

Often I went down to Gladwyn to see him and James and Susie would come also. We'd all play bridge and swim in his pool in the back yard. When Jaynie was in the hospital for a month, I went down there with Elizabeth who was a toddler at that point; I also had two little dogs I took everywhere with me. Charlie always welcomed me and whoever I had in tow—human or canine—with open arms. Partly it was because he had a maid who came in every day, so he could afford to be tolerant about having my family, but it was more that he was a loving and inclusive person.

For a few years, it was as if his house was my house. We were very seriously in love. Even though his wife was in an institution, and from what I understood from Gail not a very pleasant person, Charlie felt a great sense of duty to her and never talked about divorcing her. Despite that, he always made me feel very secure.

We traveled together quite a lot and always had a wonderful time. He was a passionate sailor and although he didn't have a boat when I knew him, he used to sail in the Bermuda races. We went to Bermuda several times where we stayed at Pink Beach in a very pleasant English hotel. On their honeymoon, James and Susie had been to Tortola, the yachting center of the Caribbean, and raved about it, so Charlie and I decided to go down there on a trip. Once we spent a week in St. Croix with his sister Marie who had a house there. I remember Marie being fun and I liked her a lot. We went to a spa in Mexico, went to Carmel and then to Olivia's graduation from Stanford Business School. Charlie introduced me to Hatchett's Point near Old Lyme, Connecticut and several summers we rented a house up there.

Wherever we stayed, he liked to play golf and I would ride along in the golf cart. Sometimes I got out and tried my swing on the putting greens. He was surprised at how good I was, although I didn't know much about the fine points of golf. Charlie was also a very good at tennis, which I had never learned how to play due to the rheumatic fever I had as a child.

James and Susie were married in 1979 and they invited Charlie to the wedding. My ex-husband didn't want to come to the wedding if Charlie was going, but my son said Charlie would be there even if his father wasn't; they wanted him there. Jim ended up coming, so they were both at the wedding making it a little bit sticky for awhile. Jim didn't join the rehearsal dinner at the beach club in Tokeneke the night before, however, but Charlie did.

The wedding weekend at my hot tub in Bedford; l-r: James, Charlie, Susie, Me, Alan Marx. (Yes, we all have bathing suits on.)

Wedding Day: Charlie, Susie, James and me.

Charlie and I had a little falling out after we had been seeing each other for probably seven or eight years. Like many people who get into arguments over money, we had some angry words and didn't see each other for a couple of months. Then we began talking on the phone again and he said, "You know I love you." He often sent me cards saying he loved me; I still have a stack of them I've kept all these years.

I was in Wisconsin and planned to stop to see him on my way back to Bedford, but I never saw him again. Charlie had said to come and stay in the house on my way back. Although he was away, I could let myself in and he'd be back in a few days. I called to see if by any chance Charlie had gotten home or to be sure nobody was there and Chuck, Jr. answered the phone, walked away and never came back to hang up the phone. I was on the road to Ohio with the two dogs and decided not to stop because his son was there. I went home and Charlie and I talked on the phone a few days later.

A few weeks later, Charlie's sister found him on his kitchen floor. He'd had a stroke and although he was still alive, he only lived another three days after they got him to the hospital. He'd had heart trouble and high blood pressure, and had been under the care of Susie's father who was a heart specialist at New York Hospital. Dr. Hinkle didn't take many new patients, but he was treating Charlie, who thought he was a terrific doctor and liked him very much.

No one called to tell me Charlie had died, probably because nobody knew we were getting back together. Henry and I were having dinner in a little restaurant in Bedford Hills and he said, "Oh, I'm sorry to hear your friend Charlie died." Totally shocked, I said, "You can't be right; it can't be true." This was about seven in the evening and the funeral was the next day. I went home immediately, told Jaynie, who was living with me, called Olivia in New York, and she said we'd all go down to the funeral. Jaynie and I drove to Brooklyn to pick up Olivia and the three of us drove down to Philadelphia that night. The girls were lovely and supportive while

I cried all the way there. We arrived early at St. David's, a very old Episcopal church out in the country with a little churchyard where Charlie and I had gone sometimes. Jaynie and I sat unobtrusively in the back, while Olivia stayed in the car.

I felt terrible for a long time. I'd wake up in the middle of the night and could hardly think of anything but Charlie. It was close to a real physical pain, and my life was totally changed for awhile. Luckily, my family was there for comfort and support since I didn't really have anything faith-based to fall back on. I wasn't angry, just terribly sad. Finally, getting busy and working hard was what pulled me through the grief of losing Charlie.

Adelaide "Addie" Docter Blodgett, 1930s.

☙ 20 ❧

Addie's Last Gift

My mother often said that I should never have any regrets about our relationship because I had always been a wonderful daughter to her; that she didn't ever want me to think that she was unhappy or that things weren't fine. I think those words are about the most generous gift a parent can give a child.

She came out from Mayville around 1984 and lived with me for a year in Bedford until she went to a nursing home only about fifteen miles away. She was very graceful about going to the home, but now that I look back on it I wonder if I should have done things differently.

Before my divorce, my mother had come to visit us often in Bedford. If I hadn't gotten divorced, it would have been easier for everybody; she would have kept coming because the house was large and accommodating. My husband was always gracious to her and my mother was sensitive, making a point of not always being around in order to give Jim and me time alone. Jim and I had dinner every night at 7:00 by candlelight and often she'd go upstairs or would eat earlier with the children.

At that time Jaynie and Elizabeth were with me along with Mother in the house I had built. I was away during the day selling real estate, and it just got to be too much for me. I had been thinking of building a room onto the house, but Mother was ninety-two, and it felt more realistic to set her up in a home. The home I found was a lovely old colonial set on a hilltop near the Hudson River. It had a large veranda, high ceilings, and was only for women. I tried to go see Mother once a week; sometimes she came back to the house with me, and often I'd take her out for a ride to do things like get a hearing aide or go to a doctor's appointment. My children also visited her when they came home. The home was a decent, comfortable place where she had her own room, but I can see how it must have been hard for her. She never once complained, or made me feel guilty.

Then she fell. They thought she might have broken a hip so she went to the hospital, but amazingly hadn't broken any bones. We were about to take her out of the hospital and put her in a more intensive care facility when she fell again. She complained about pain inside and the doctor thought she had some internal bleeding. We had to decide right away whether an invasive exploratory operation should be done. Fortunately Bill had come to visit her, so he and Margaret were already at my house and able to help with the decision, which was incredibly difficult to make. Given her age of ninety-seven, we decided not to put her through the operation, but it felt as if we were pulling the plug on her. Jaynie and Olivia made it out to Mayville in time to see her before she died.

I have a letter my mother wrote to Santa Claus eighty-eight years earlier when she was nine. What her spelling and grammar lack, her penmanship more than makes up for—every letter beautifully formed, meticulously executed—just as she taught me when I was close to nine years old. To me, it shows the essence of who she was—unselfish, communicative, concerned with others, positive and loving. That was my mother, Addie Docter.

Mayville, Wisconsin, December
12, 1901. Mr. Santa Claus.
Dear Mr. Santa Claus.
I will have a good time on
Christmas morning.
Please bring me a sled and
a dresser and a christmas
tree.
My mamma and papa is
working every day.
We are going to have an enter-
tainment in our school and
we all will try to enjoy our
selfs and I suppose you will
enjoy your self to. So good by.
                    Your truly
                    Addie Doctor

❧ 21 ❧
Losing Gloria

A round the time I got married, Gloria moved to Philadelphia and started working for *The Philadelphia In-
quirer.* After a few years she moved back to New York
where she was hired by *The Herald Tribune,* and then *The
New York Times.* Gloria went with Langdon for seven or
eight years, but it was always so traumatic—living a social
whirlwind in both New York and Washington—that she
never married him. In a couple of letters she wrote how
Langdon wanted to get married, but by that point she had
decided he was too unpredictable. She married twice, but
never had any children, I imagine by choice.

When Gloria lived in New York she used to come out
to Bedford occasionally. She was very fond of my children
who only remember her slightly because they were quite
young at the time.

During the next couple of decades while I was married
and raising my children I saw her sporadically, but it was
really our letter writing that kept us in touch. Just as in our

New York days, we continued to be each other's sounding board and confidant. I've kept Gloria's letters all these years.

In 1956 Gloria had visited Saigon. At that time, the Vietnamese capital was a beautiful, alive place, which she adored. She was then hired by *The New York Times* in the women's news department, but after four years of writing about clothes, she became restless, and in 1960 abruptly left the paper. Four years later, *The Times* begged her to come back to cover high fashion in Paris, which she agreed to do. In Paris she met many Vietnamese exiles seeking refuge from the war, and became passionately involved in their plight. Having spent time in Saigon, she requested *The Times* send her to Vietnam to write about the terrible changes in the Vietnamese peoples' lives, something that the large press corps there didn't touch upon, since they were so busy covering the military story.

Before she went back to Vietnam, I went to see her in Paris where she was covering the spring fashions. We spent a couple of days together and I remember we were going around singing "*...those were the days, my friend, I thought they'd never end...*" reminiscing about Langdon and Jack Kennedy and our more innocent times in New York. Here I was in the throes of divorce and a faltering affair with Harold, and Gloria was about to take off to a dangerous, war torn country. Our lives had taken very different paths, but we were still deep friends.

Gloria was an amazing person. I didn't agree with her politics, but I admired her courage. She wasn't just a reporter; she basically became the United States' conscience about the Vietnam War, reporting on the impact the war had not only on the lives of American soldiers, but also on the Vietnamese people. Gloria was never afraid to speak out and her words were searing and passionate. She wrote about false body counts, declared that high US military officials were lying, explored the use of hard drugs by American soldiers and, with great compassion, wrote about the reasons for their drug abuse. She wrote passionately about the tragedy and bravery of the Vietnamese people, whom many Americans didn't even think about anymore, much less their own men being sent off to the slaughter of war. One of her most powerful ideas was that Americans were "killing at a distance," which enabled people back home to have little consciousness or to care about the immense suffering we were causing. She maintained that no matter what the military said, the war was anything but noble; that it was inflicting endless "physical suffering and psychic damage" on Vietnamese civilians and both Vietnamese and American soldiers. She insisted it was important for war zones to be covered by female correspondents because "at heart, men are boys, easily dazzled by guns and uniforms."

People used to say there was no more accomplished female war correspondent at that time than Gloria Emerson. She won awards for excellence in foreign reporting. Knowing Gloria, I imagine she was deeply disturbed by people's ability to rationalize the horror of the Vietnam War, and she took it personally, which is what made her so passionate.

The last time I saw Gloria was when I ran into her accidentally at Bonwit Tellers. By then she was a correspondent in Vietnam. She was rushing off to some book affair where she was either speaking or getting an award, and I never saw her after that. We had already started to lose touch around the time I was getting divorced. Over the next decade I was so involved trying to get my real estate career off the ground, along with trying to manage my own challenging family affairs that I didn't go into New York to see Gloria when she wasn't in Vietnam. I saw her on television one time quite by accident on a late night interview program; I also had the recording of the notoriously contentious interview she did with John Lennon and Yoko Ono, *Imagine John Lennon*", where she challenged them on the effectiveness of their anti-war actions.

I tried to find Gloria around 2000, but it wasn't as easy then as it would be now using the internet. *The New York Times* wouldn't give out addresses; they'd only leave a message for her, and I was never sure she was getting my messages. It's possible she didn't want to see me because of her illness, which I didn't know about then. I suppose I could have gotten a private detective to find her, but that seemed extreme. Anyway, I never found her and I really regret not having worked harder at it, making the effort to go into New York, even camping out at *The New York Times* to wait for her. All I know is she was a huge part of my life, and I would have loved to connect with her again in those years.

Gloria died in 2004 by suicide. She was found by friends alone in her apartment in New York, and had written her own obituary. Apparently she had even told some friends that she was going to commit suicide, but as I said before, she could be very dramatic. In our younger, wilder years, I think she did things for effect, but at the end she really did commit suicide.

She had been diagnosed with Parkinson's Disease and I imagine couldn't envision her life without being able to write, not to mention becoming a total invalid and having to be taken care of. Parkinson's Disease led to degeneration of the brain and ultimately lack of motor control. This was not Gloria.

I would like to contact some of her friends in New York and talk further about her and what happened. It remains an incomplete chapter in my life, which I would like to feel more at peace with.

LOSING GLORIA

Me on the boat to Guilin. 1987.

☜ 22 ☞

"Life is Not Always Boring"

Elizabeth was my first granddaughter, and I got to see a fair amount of her since she and Jaynie lived with me off and on throughout her childhood. When she was old enough, I took her on trips with me. Elizabeth is the one who made up the name "Nonie," which all my granddaughters call me.

James' job with Chase took him all over the world. The year after he and Susie were married they lived in Brooklyn Heights, but the following year moved to Paris and lived various places abroad until 2008. I visited them regularly wherever they were, so I could know Sarah, Emily and Abby while they were growing up. Usually they made a trip to see me once a year, so I didn't feel as deprived as I could have!

One summer when they visited me in Narrowsburg, New York, they created a play called "Life is Not Always Boring," produced by the three of them along with a friend.

That's where Sarah made her acting debut. The invitation shows a map of where the play would take place, and asked the audience to "Please be indulgent and we hope you will enjoy this play." They were always doing creative, imaginative things like that.

Matching sundresses bought by Olivia. l-r: my niece Mindy Blodgett, Olivia, Elizabeth.1980s

I took Elizabeth with me twice to Paris. James' and Susie's apartment in Paris was on the Avenue du President Kennedy, and if you hung out over the balcony, you could see the Eiffel Tower. One weekend we went to Normandy, which was just beautiful, especially the picturesque little harbor we visited called Les Andeles. James and Susie took us to an ancient castle that they loved to share with visitors, and we spent the night nearby in a lovely inn where they had stayed before.

The next place they moved was Hong Kong where they lived for seven years. Hong Kong was fabulous, and one time when I went with Elizabeth, we took a hovercraft to Macau and back. Several times we got a junk for the day—a perk for the people working in the bank (even clerks could reserve them). The junks had two boat boys who made lunch, served and waited on us, as we sailed around the islands. At times the boat would stop, so the girls could jump off a diving board and swim. It was like being on a yacht, and we had a fabulous time.

On another visit to China we made a trip into the interior to a place called Guilin, which was one of the most beautiful places I've ever seen. Its dramatic tall, rounded hills were the inspiration for typical Chinese landscape paintings.

James was transferred to London in 1991. When I visited there, again with Elizabeth, I took all four girls to Windsor Castle for the day. We went on a great little tour, including seeing the princess' dollhouse and the royal chapel where Queen Elizabeth's father King George was buried. I loved the quote on his tomb, so I stood there laboriously copying it, only to find it printed on a card when I went into the gift shop. As a matter of fact, I have it in my will that it should be read at my funeral. I just love the way it sounds:

I said to the man who stood at the gate of the Year, "Give me a light that I may tread safely into the unknown." And he replied, "Go out into the darkness and put your hand into the hand of God. That shall be to you better than light and safer than a known way!"

-Minnie Louise Haskins

*Christmas in Hong Kong
Clockwise from top: Susie, James, Abby, Sarah, Emily.*

James left Chase in London to join Visa in Singapore where they lived for eleven years. They returned to the US in 2008 having lived abroad for twenty-seven years. The girls were in schools here, and James and Susie wanted to be closer to them and their parents.

James and Susie just celebrated their 30th wedding anniversary. They told me recently that they had had a ceremony to repeat their vows. When I asked who was going to officiate they told me Sarah had become an ordained minister and performed the ceremony!

JAYNE BLODGETT MURRAY

༄ 23 ༄

Midlife Peregrinations

A little blurb in a newspaper I received called *Human Events* talked about a trip to Eastern Europe under the auspices of the Conservative Caucus, led by Howard Philips. He was the Constitution Party's candidate for president of the United States in the 1992, 1996 and 2000 elections. It would be a small group of people, and the main theme of the trip was to explore anti-Communist issues in meetings with various conservative heads of governments and political parties. It was a subject I was extremely interested in, plus I felt it was a time when I could easily go. I enjoyed it so much that I took two more trips under the same organization.

Eastern Europe, 1990

This trip encompassed Yugoslavia, East Germany, Poland, Hungary, Czechoslovakia, and Romania all in only two weeks. I didn't go with anybody I knew, but met many wonderful people in our group including Pat Buchanan, his wife, and his sister Babe, who sometimes sits on TV panels. Pat is on a show I watch every morning, and I enjoy his commentary a lot. On the trip, I met a man named Jack Anderson who published *Farm and Ranch Magazine,* which had quite a large circulation at the time. He was very conservative and had a great sense of humor—a very, very funny man. He's made many recordings of his talks, which he laces with humor, so they're not only informative but very entertaining. We often sat together on the bus, and I thoroughly enjoyed his company.

The routine was to get up at 5:30 in the morning, meet for breakfast and spend all morning and into the afternoon listening to speeches and meeting people. I always enjoyed the talks and took copious notes. I admit sometimes I got sleepy because it was quite intensive, but it was a great challenge to keep focused on what was said. The best thing about a tour like this was that everyone was interested in the same things, and we all loved talking about what we heard. We used to meet around large conference tables where we could ask questions of various people. In the afternoons after the discussions, we often went on walking tours to get to know the city we were in. In the evening, Howard always scheduled a nice place to have dinner, followed by another speaker. We ended the evening with an inspiring concert or other cultural event.

We flew from New York and landed in Zagreb where we were met at the hotel by a group of violinists—and champagne. In Belgrade we met with Franjo Tudman, the first president of Croatia. I have a photo of one of the hotels we stayed at in Yugoslavia where the cement was crumbling and falling off, but we happened to be there the first day they got their flag back. We had brought a lot of American flag pins with us, which we passed out to the local children who were so happy to get these little American flags along with their own. People were all out on their balconies, watching their flag, which had its star back on; it was really very touching.

When I was in Berlin, they were just starting to tear the Berlin Wall down. You could rent a hammer and take a whack at it yourself or buy a hunk with grafitti on it. I felt very good about The Wall coming down, as did most of the world, I think. It felt as if it could be the beginning of the end of the aftermath of the Communist order, which was starting to break down. Berlin had been rebuilt and there were things that were more advanced than what we had. The bathrooms were so modern that we couldn't figure out how to flush the toilets, which became the subject of several dinner conversations—everyone comparing notes as to whether they had figured out how to flush yet.

In Berlin we met with Bill Mittendorf, the ambassador to Germany, and we also met with the managing director of the Deutsches Bank.

Howard arranged for dinner in a charming old restaurant at a lovely hotel on the outskirts of Berlin, an absolutely beautiful place where I'd love to stay someday. From one point in the city, we looked out over the area where Hitler's bunker was supposed to have been. We saw the Brandenberg Gate, not yet liberated from the Wall.

At a cocktail party reception in Wroclaw, Poland we met the Cardinal of Poland, the head of the Catholic Church there in the Catholic headquarters.

Prague is an absolutely beautiful city. There we met the finance minister and Vaclav Klaus, then the prime minister of the Czech Republic. We took a wonderful walking tour of Prague, saw the famous clock and a Jewish cemetery in the center of the city. The cemetery is not very large and bodies had been buried thirteen deep on top of each other for several centuries. They just layered them. This was a very sacred spot for Jewish people.

Budapest was amazing because of its architecture, the River Danube, and its bridges connecting Bude on one side and Pest on the other. We stayed in a hotel on the Danube, directly across from the Houses of Parliament where we had meetings in a conference room.

In Romania, we were met just over the border with champagne. The people were so glad to have us, and were very welcoming. One of the highlights was visiting some caves where we had dinner, and later folk dances were performed for us. Then we went to Timisasoara, the main economic and cultural center in western Romania, which was like a desert. Romania was the poorest country I've ever seen.

I received the following certification after completing the trip:

The Conservative Caucus Research, Analysis and Education Foundation certifies that Jayne B. Murray has with good humor, patience, and determination, completed the requisite regimen of airline aggravation, hard travel, intensive indoctrination, luminous reading, daily discipline, sleep deprivation, border crawling, gastronomical aggression, to successfully survive and qualify as a graduate of Howard Philips' Eastern Europe 1990 Tour with tours of the cities of Zagreb, Kravazky, Berlin, Warclaw, Praha and Bratislava, Ochenska, Slovenska, Budapest, and Belgrade.

The Baltic Liberation Tour, 1991

The following year I took the Baltic Liberation Tour in which we went to Poland, Latvia, Lithuania and Estonia. The first secretary of the Latvian litigation talked to us before we left, flying first to Helsinki and from there to Warsaw. There we saw a Polish folkloric performance, had a briefing with Polish journalists about the situation in Poland, and met with members of various political parties, like the Central Alliance Party, at their headquarters. We toured the old town in Warsaw where we saw the old market square and the place where survivors of the Nazi occupation rebuilt their city.

From Warsaw we took a Soviet train to Vilnius, Lithuania. It had been advertised as a luxury train, and one of the reasons I decided to take that trip was because I thought it would be such fun to take a Soviet luxury train, which I imagined would be like the Orient Express that Jim and I had taken on our honeymoon, with its beautiful paneling and old fashioned décor.

Our group was to have two sleeping cars. We were told we'd be served breakfast on board, but to bring along a snack. When we got on board we found out there wasn't any dining car; instead of an elegant decor, the train was very run down and grubby, with dirty curtains that looked like pieces of old sheets sagging over the windows. The bathrooms were incredibly primitive and dirty. There were shared compartments with beds like hard boards covered with very thin mattresses and skimpy blankets.

In the middle of the night the train stopped. Soldiers in britches and big heavy boots boarded, walked right into our compartments without even knocking and looked at our jewelry. It was really kind of scary because they were very stern, almost Nazi types.

Then the wheels had to be switched because the gauge of the track changed between countries, a safety measure implemented after World War I in order to make the borders more secure. With different track gauges, trains had to stop at the border to make the change, preventing one country from rushing into another with a train full of troops to take over. We watched as they raised the cars, unscrewed and removed the wheels, leaving a huge hole in the bottom of each end of the car until they screwed the other ones in. We didn't know at the time that Howard Phillips was taken off the train with his son who was helping him on this trip. They had some literature and gifts for the conservative party people with whom we were meeting during our tours. The soldiers took them to the police station and questioned Howard for a couple of hours. We were delayed, but it was kind of exciting.

There wasn't a thing to eat. The only thing in the morning was tea, served in teacups in the metal holders like they have throughout Europe. I stole one, feeling totally justified after such dashed expectations for an elegant train!

In Latvia we went to Riga, a port second only to Leningrad, where we heard a late afternoon concert in a Lutheran Cathedral, world-renowned for its 6,768 pipe organ. We toured an ethnographic museum, much like our Williamsburg, with people dressed in costume, to get a feel for what life was like for the peasants in Latvia. It was interesting because people in Latvia are very Scandinavian looking; there are many blonds in Latvia, Lithuania and Estonia.

People dressed in folk costumes did wonderful dances out by a lake. Latvia has a big music festival that almost everybody attends, since there aren't that many people in the entire country. They all come and sing; clearly they love music.

The tour was wonderful because we got to see out-of-the-way places, like Talin, a medieval city in Estonia that most visitors don't ever get to visit. We had one of the writers from *National Review* and a writer for the *Washington Merry-Go-Round* speak to us, and heard a man who presented a dialogue between Jews and Poles. Actually, Howard Philips is of Jewish background, but converted to Catholicism.

Most of the people of Estonia are Greek Orthodox. We were there on a Sunday, and went inside a church, which had bullet holes in the walls where people had recently been killed. The church was beautiful; everything looked almost gilded. Mostly elderly women attended the service, and since there were no seats, everybody stood. The music was just gorgeous.

This time I earned a Magna cum Laude certificate for this challenging but fabulous tour!

Jayne Murray, having survived a historic nice day walk through history, focusing on how a) the peoples of Poland and America pay the bill for western bank loans for communist despots, and b) the brave residents of the Baltic

Republic endure unrelenting intimidation, harassment and deprivation from armed Soviet intruders; having experienced KGB assisted border crossings, sleepless nights, speech filled days and self-serve sanitation systems not yet penetrated by Peristroika, *the above named honoree is duly designated a Magna cum Laude graduate.*

A New World Order, 1993

I couldn't wait to go on yet another trip with this organization. In 1993, I joined the tour called "A New World Order," which took us to England. "A new world order" is kind of a Communist phrase, which you hear a lot now in political commentary if you start listening for it. The Nazis had been fighting for a new world order. It's remaking the world into more of a socialist system, which we were opposed to. Howard Philips gave the title to this tour because we were looking at the side that opposes the New World Order in the countries we visited.

On that trip that we did more financial things, such as going to the Bank of London. In England we had an entrée into places like the Houses of Parliament. We were able to go to the House of Commons, and sit in the seat where the prime minister sits because we had a member of the House of Parliament with us who was a friend of Howard's. We also went to the United Nations headquarters in The Netherlands where we had a meeting in one of the boardrooms of the World Bank.

Cringletie House

❧ 24 ❧

The Murray Nose and the Blodgett Nose

O ne of my favorite trips was when Olivia and I drove through Scotland in 1990. We stopped in London where we stayed with my friend Cynthia Fletcher and the next day took a train to Edinburgh. We rented a car and drove around Scotland for ten days, staying at some really lovely inns and discovered, totally by accident, another piece of the Murray family history.

I hadn't liked Scotland the first time I was there on my honeymoon, but on this trip I fell in love with it. Although it was cold and rainy, I couldn't get enough of the beauty of the Scottish lowlands. The highlands were equally gorgeous, but in a different way. During wet weather, waterfalls in the highlands just poured out of the moors and you could hear them all around you. Everything was s a lush, wonderful green, and when we got out to walk on the moors the ground was spongy. It looked like one would imagine the mountains of the moon would look, only with waterfalls.

Not too far from Edinburgh, Olivia and I stumbled on Cringletie House. We saw a long driveway that wound through lovely, well-groomed grounds and drove in. At the end of the driveway was a grand country house with unusual, small towers at the corners of the top floor, almost like a castle. We were amazed to see on the outside of the wall the Murray coat of arms! We were dying to stay there, but they didn't have room for us that night. A few days later when we drove back we tried again and got a room.

The Cringletie is a beautiful little hotel, and as it turns out, was once owned by Sir James Wolfe Murray. The first house at Cringletie was built in 1666, but over the next two centuries it became so dilapidated that Sir James rebuilt it in 1861. Olivia and I knew nothing of this when we first came upon it. With only fifteen rooms, it felt very intimate, and as we entered our room, there was a huge fruit basket welcoming us. On the main floor was a lovely sitting room where guests went before dinner for a Scotch and some friendly conversation.

Behind the house was a huge walled garden, famous throughout the border area, with an amazing yew hedge that's at least four hundred years old—some people claim the oldest in Scotland. There was also an herb and vegetable garden where they grew food served in the restaurant. Another part had an orchard and a fruit cage that protected emerging fruit from birds and other animals.

Over the years, the current owners have been improving the grounds, planting trees and thousands of daffodil bulbs, building woodland walks, and restoring the walled garden. Guests are free to wander all over the acres of sweeping lawns scattered with grazing sheep, woods, areas where you can play pitch and putt, croquet, and boules. There's a gorgeous waterfall and a historic dovecote. It's all incredibly uplifting.

There was a painting in the sitting room that I photographed because it looked so much like James. It was very similar to the portrait at the top of my stairs here, of Dr. John Murray, who lived in Norwich, England in the 1700s. James looks so much like him also. He has the Murray nose. It's interesting to see the resemblance so many generations back and an ocean away!

I loved Cringletie House so much that I've been back several times and want to go again. I took James and Susie there when they were living in England several years after my first visit, and went again with Elizabeth when I took her to Scotland one May on the John Jay Homestead Garden Club Tour. It was a tour with the Garden Club of Bedford where a group of about fourteen ladies went to the Royal Flower Show. I rented a car and Elizabeth and I drove down to visit Cringletie House.

ᴄꙅ

Not to be outdone by the Murray Nose, there seems to be the equally compelling feature of the Blodgett Nose. Here's a letter that I received from a relative up in Concord, New Hampshire, one of those people like me who loves to do lineage also. I got in touch with him when I was doing my genealogy research for the DAR. He said one of the unexpected bonuses in his search for Blodgetts has been the friendships that have developed.

Much as I enjoy having your photo I do have one regret. I wish your picture was larger, as I would like to have had a larger picture of your nose. Did you know most Blodgett's have noses? A year ago two ladies came to my door. I knew they were coming so I greeted them with 'Ladies, not a word until I tell you which of you is the Blodgett.' The nose did it. We have a portrait of my wife's mother who was born a Blodgett, I also have a photograph of a miniature painting of the famous or notorious Samuel who was so instrumental in establishing Washington D.C., that's the one in that picture there. These two photos of people 100 years apart, and as distantly related as possible, have absolutely identical noses. I'm not quite sure about you, maybe you join my wife in being one of the black sheep of the family. Oh yes, you will want to know what I am talking about. There is a definitely shaped little hump or outward curve in the nose perhaps a little higher up than most humps. Not at all a disturbing feature. I think I have well over 100 instances of recognizable noses. What an interesting example for the proper scientist. Thanks again for thinking of me.

For the record, I never liked my nose. When I smile, I think it always gets too wide. Additionally for the record, my granddaughter Sarah doesn't like her nose either.

Part IV

cs

Narrowsburg: 1993-1998

Christmas at the Commodore Murray House.
Me, Daisy and Elizabeth..

25

The Commodore Murray House

O f all the houses I've had, my grandchildren liked The Commodore Murray House the best.

I always loved looking through the luxury homes section of *The New York Times*. and one Sunday in 1993 when I was up at Hatchet's Point, The Commodore Murray House caught my eye, mostly because of the name. It looked like a southern colonial, and the minimal words described it as a "4,000 square foot mansion on 2.3 acres with 300 feet of Delaware River frontage." Between the name and the fact that it was on a river—happily reminding me of my childhood on the Rock River—Olivia and I decided that we should drive up and take a look at it. I knew we had no relationship to Commodore Chauncey Murray, who, by the way, was not a military man. "Commodore" was his first name. I didn't expect to buy it; I just wanted to see it.

The house was in the hamlet of Narrowsburg, about 125 miles north of New York City where the Delaware River cuts through the mountains—the Catskills in New York and the Poconos in Pennsylvania. It was right on the river on the New York side.

Both Olivia and I loved the house, which dated back to 1830s. Originally it was a private residence that changed ownership a few times. Known as French Renaissance Revival Second Empire, it had three dormer windows, double balconies in the front with beautifully decorated balustrades and a Mansard roof. It had an unusual sunken living room, cherry wood paneling throughout, a formal dining room with four French doors, two openings onto the wraparound porch, six bedrooms, and three bathrooms, one of which had a lovely view of the river and bridge from the tub.

The Commodore Murray House and the Carriage House (left).

It only took us two visits to envision morning coffee or a glass of wine in the evening on the verandah that stretched the full length of the house. The view was spectacular. The deep lawn, with mature oaks and maples, fruit trees and lilac bushes, dropped about twelve feet to the river. Close by was a little island within rowing distance. In direct view was the Narrowsburg Bridge, which carried the interstate between Pennsylvania and New York at the river's narrowest point—hence the name Narrowsburg. The river funneled through this narrow part and swirled into the widest and deepest part—what's known as the Big Eddy. Over a hundred years ago, raftsmen driving thousands of logs down the river would tie up here, stop into Commodore Murray's eatery and spend the night.

During the golden age of railroads, the Erie chugged through Narrowsburg, dropping New Yorkers eager to escape the oppressive heat of the city and enjoy the summer in the cool mountains. Through the years, the Commodore Murray went through several identities—alternately a store, a hotel until 1887, a launch and sandwich shop for a boat livery, and a restaurant. Once it was broken into apartments, then reunified.

The Commodore Murray would make a fabulous bed and breakfast and that's exactly what I intended to do. I bought the mansion from George and Alice Moore, moved in in November of 1993 and spent the winter redecorating, using my favorite style of marrying elegance and comfort. I filled the house with antiques I had picked up along the way, hung Grandpa's photographs and the old portraits from Jim's family, and showcased the melodeon and the dollhouse that had belonged to my mother. I repainted the living room a rich, chocolate brown and the dining room a dark red. I decorated the four guest rooms with treasures I'd collected in my travels. Once open for business, I always put fresh flowers and chocolates in the guests' rooms.

As if the 4,000-square-foot mansion weren't enough, there was also a restored post and beam carriage house, the second floor of which was a 900-square-foot artist's studio with high ceilings and lovely maple floors.

The only imperfection to my idyllic country mansion was the unsightly bridge right in the middle of my view. It was a terrible grey color with huge patches of peeling paint, jarring against the vibrant green of the trees. It had a fairly long span, certainly not a narrow bridge like the footbridge in Mayville, so was prominent in my otherwise spectacular view. Since my guests and I looked at it every day, I thought I'd like to get it painted. I was on the city Chamber of Commerce and I proposed the project. It was a very complicated process since I had to go through both the Pennsylvania and New York governments, due to the fact that all bridges on the Delaware are divided between states. The River Masters control the water level and the Delaware is a *very* controlled river. Anyway, the Highway Departments of New York and Pennsylvania agreed that the bridge did need painting since it hadn't been done in fifteen years. I made sure I got on the committee that would decide the color because I didn't want it painted the usual rust or battle ship grey. I wanted it green to blend in with the trees. Since there were only a couple of other people on the committee besides me and they didn't particularly care what color it would be, I got the green I wanted.

It cost about a million dollars to paint that bridge and took the entire summer. First they had to scrape off the previous lead paint, so the bridge was shrouded in canvass and the painters had to wear zipper suits to protect them from the lead.

Anyway, I got the bridge painted which made my view so much better. When one of my guests remarked how lovely it would be to have lights on the bridge, I started working on that. I got lights on either end, which was also a very complicated process because the authorities had to decide whether the power was going to come out of Pennsylvania or New York.

Unfortunately, the bridge and the eddy had a tragic side. One year a dead body floated up about seventy feet from my dock. Two twenty-year-old boys had been swimming near the bridge where the current is stronger and more dangerous than it looks, especially in spring. Because of the whirlpool effect of the eddy, one boy got pulled under; the other jumped in to try to save him and was also pulled under. This happened almost every year—someone would get caught in the current, pulled down 120 feet, where they'd stay for a day or two before surfacing. On this particular occasion, they had helicopters and the fire department rescue crew looking right in front of my house for the boys for almost two days before one of them rose. I can't remember where they found the other, but it was tragic.

The Narrowsburg Bridge

I spent five years in Narrowsburg, occasionally going down to Bedford to keep my hand in with the real estate business. I became somewhat involved in the community, doing things like getting flower baskets put up in town, and I kept busy with my guests. People came to Narrowsburg to go rafting and fishing, see bald eagles and other birds, and enjoy the fall colors. It was an easy getaway from New York City, an escape into nature without much traveling.

In 1997 I decided to sell The Commodore Murray and move back to Bedford. The house was a bit of a hard sell because the area was somewhat depressed and the town of Narrowsburg a bit too artsy for most people. It was also a very small town and there really wasn't much there.

Just as I was getting ready to leave Narrowsburg, Daisy came shyly wagging into my life. I had the house up for sale, and a woman from New York who came to look at it told me in passing that she had seven beagle puppies needing homes. I hadn't really planned to get a dog yet, but Elizabeth was coming to stay with me, and I thought it would be nice for her to have a dog. I loved beagles. I called the woman and said I'd like to buy one. She didn't want to charge me because the puppies didn't have papers; in fact, they were not pure-breds but half beagle and half sheltie. Always wanting to give the "underdog" a chance, I told her I'd take the female runt of the litter.

The woman drove the hundred and twenty miles to deliver the puppy. When I saw her, I was disappointed because she had more of a sheltie face than beagle face, plus she was so timid that she just hid under the dining room table, terrified to go out onto the porch or the lawn. I guess she had never seen grass before. I almost thought I was going to have to give her away because she was so fearful. My cleaning woman liked her a lot and said she'd be glad to take her, but I knew they lived on the main street and had a ten-year-old boy. I thought I couldn't let Daisy go to that situation.

Daisy in her youth.

It only took me a week to get attached to her despite her issues. There was the little problem of whenever someone came to the door, she got excited and left a puddle. That got better until eventually she only did it when someone came to the door *and* tried to pat her on the head. We worked through that, and gradually she emerged from her shyness to be my special and loving dog.

Part V

❧

Mayville: 2000 –

Companions on the steps of White Limestone School. The Mayville News, *2008. Photo by Sally Kahlhamer.*

❦ 26 ❧

Full Circle

*H*ere I am back in Mayville, having been away for over fifty years. I live on the same street I grew up on and look out my window at the same bend in the river I loved as a little girl. Often people are curious why I moved back to Mayville after so many years in and around the sophistication of New York; others think it's the most natural thing in the world to return to one's roots.

I had rented out my house in Bedford while I was in Narrowsburg, so still had it when I decided to return to Bedford. I had kept my real estate license in case I decided to buy a house, since I could use it as a discount through another broker. I only gave my license up a few years ago, partly because it was costing me $400 a year and I was no longer using it.

After a couple of years back in Bedford, I visited Mayville over Christmas to see how I liked it, opening myself to the possibility of moving back and starting a B & B there. I had been going into the real estate office occasionally, but had begun to think, why should I keep working in New York State and pay the high taxes? I also felt real estate was getting way too technical. You had to use a cell phone, do listings and check the houses by computer. It was no longer informal and personal. I decided I didn't want to keep up with it all; I probably could have, but basically I just don't like computers. I was also thinking I had no idea where any of my children were really going to settle. James was living abroad, Olivia was living and working in New York, and Jaynie had moved up to Danbury. Dear friends like Charlie and Helen had died, and I realized I didn't have any deep connection to Bedford anymore.

That Christmas of 2000, Mayville felt welcoming and familiar, so I decided to move back. Even though I didn't have any relatives living here anymore, I could still feel the strong family connections. It was comforting to hear people say they had heard of my grandfather, or that they remembered my mother and her reputation for kindness in the community. I re-met quite a few people I had gone to school with, or who had known my brother.

So I packed up nearly fifty years of my life, shipped the melodeon once again from New York to Wisconsin, and drove back as I had done so many summers with my children. This time Daisy was my co-pilot, easy company as only a dog can be.

Running the bed and breakfast in Narrowsburg had been a fun and rewarding time for me, and I thought why not do it here? I bought a house on North German Street, right across from my childhood home. It was an old Victorian, which I renovated, starting with installing skylights to let in more light. I created a bedroom out of the attic, made a few other changes, and opened it as a Bed & Breakfast.

Then the Carter's house came on the market. They had owned it for forty years. I'd always liked it as a child when the Reading family owned it, and I walked past it up the street from where I lived. The house had four floors, five bedrooms and four bathrooms—unheard of for any house in

Mayville during the Depression. Out back, closer to the river, was a little one-room summer cottage with a fireplace, which the Reading girls used to invite me over to play in. I thought what a terrific bed and breakfast the house would make, especially with all the people who come to see the Horicon Marsh.

The house dates back to 1883 and was originally a substantial Victorian brick structure with 30-inch thick foundation walls. In the 1920s, Gustav Reading, then its owner, transformed it into the English manor-style mansion he felt would be worthy of his grand economic ambitions. He had founded the Wisconsin Radiator Furniture Corporation, was a hugely successful salesman, and had set up a manufacturing facility on Horicon Street. Supervising every detail in the construction of the house and sparing no expense, he skillfully absorbed the original structure into his expanded Tudor Revival home, a style popular at the time along Milwaukee's lakefront.

I love the old house's history and character. Its exterior exudes grandness and solidity, with its mixture of stone and weeping mortared brick. It sits on an acre, with large, very old trees and three hundred feet of gorgeous riverfront. Inside, I've tried to create an atmosphere of simultaneous elegance and coziness. I'm a romanticist in my interior decorating; I like to create moods and surroundings that make people feel comfortable. One of the most important elements is lighting, which sets the mood. Gentle, ambient light. It bothers me when people come in and flip on a bright overhead light, which totally ruins the atmosphere, so I try to go ahead and have a soft light turned on, which makes a room look welcoming. Lighting is everything. Besides, we all look better in dim light!

Lots of multi-paned, diamond-shaped leaded glass casement windows offer views of the river out the back. Out the front you can see other historic homes on North German Street. Hand-hewn oak beams and deep crown moldings top nine-foot high ceilings in the living room, and a big stone

*Thanksgiving, 2008; l-r: my granddaughters Abby,
Sarah, Emily in my living room in Mayville.*

fireplace that I spend hours in front of on winter evenings, anchors the room. Recently I put in a gas burning fixture that makes the fire easy to light. There are beautiful old oak floors throughout the house and wrought iron railings inside and out. When the kitchen was remodeled in the 1950s, a bay window was added, giving a wide angled view of the river. My guests, first cup of morning coffee in hand, seem to congregate there while I'm cooking their breakfast, enjoying the view no matter what season. I spend a lot of time in my cozy library with its floor to ceiling bookshelves on one wall and family photos, many taken by my grandfather, filling the other walls.

There's a large master bedroom and three guest bedrooms on the second floor. The third floor has what must have originally been the maid's room with French toille wallpaper, and back stairs leading directly to the kitchen. There's also a garret with an amazing bird's eye view of the river, a bathroom with a clawfoot tub and a large room which was added in the 1970s to serve as an office. The semi-basement "game room" with its elegant flagstone floor has French doors with original windows that open out to the expanse of lawn sloping to the river. A cobblestone driveway leads from the street alongside the house to the garage. On a summer's evening, I love to sit out on the back patio, built with Cream City bricks salvaged from a torn-down gas station, and look out at the river.

I've filled the house with family antiques, old portraits, Grandpa's photos and meaningful things I've acquired during my lifetime and my travels. The melodeon has a place of honor in the hallway where people first come in. The same vase my mother always had on the melodeon sits in the exact same spot she used to put it and, like her, I always keep it filled with whatever flowers are available at the farmers' market. The pastel of the little boy I did at the age of ten hangs on a dining room wall. In the living room is a large oil painting of Maria Bronson, Jim's great grandmother, by George Peter Alexander Healey, whose portrait of Abraham Lincoln hangs in the White House. In the upstairs hallway, a portrait of Dr. John Murray sporting the Murray nose hangs above the chest that Chip, James' family dog, chewed the leg off of the week after he arrived from Singapore.

Between the main house and the river still stands the doll's house cottage. By the time I bought River's Bend Inn, my granddaughters were too old to enjoy playing in it, but often the neighbors' children come over to play.

In 2004, I added a small house to The River's Bend Inn guest options. It sits on a piece of land down by the river that abuts my acre. Built in the early 1960s, it's got definite Frank Lloyd Wright overtones: a cement slab and a flat roof leave no spaces to accumulate clutter (Wright's biggest fear), but most importantly, it has a feeling of oneness with nature. The living room has large bank of windows slanted rather uniquely inward from top to bottom, allowing an incredible view north of the expanse of lawn and the Rock River, stunning in any season.

View of the Rock River from my yard.

The previous owners had lost the house to foreclosure and left it in complete disarray—garbage all over the place, every surface encrusted with grime and cigarette smoke; just the most awful mess. It took two days to drag out all the rubbish and scour the surfaces before we could begin to rehabilitate the structure. I replaced all the doors, enlarged the windows to let in more light, and put in French doors, which always add so much character and atmosphere. The entire renovation was an enormous undertaking, and I couldn't have done it without Dennis Hintz's knowledge and expertise.

I wanted to create a sort of north woods cabin feeling, so I have wildlife prints and forest scenes all over the walls. It all ties together, even though I used different kinds of materials like string art, 1920s black velvet paintings, mid-20th Century furniture, and modern decorative accents. I got most of the art and furnishings from a second hand shop called Bethesda in Horicon. The whole process was like one of those TV home decorating shows where you see people raiding houses and doing the most decorating they can with limited funds. That's what I did for the "annex" and had great fun doing it.

Sometimes people wonder why I have a poster of Jack Kennedy, looking young and innocent, in one of the bedrooms along with all the wildlife art. Only rarely do I tell the truth; usually I just say, smiling to myself, "Oh, I just loved Jack Kennedy." Let them think I mean politically!

Sitting in the living room, looking out the bank of windows, you can see the old brewery across the river and the old stones edging the riverbank. You could be in Italy or just about any exotic place in the world. The house is so quiet and peaceful.

03

I thoroughly enjoy the people who stay at bed and breakfasts; they tend to love historical things. Of course, here in Mayville, people come also to visit the Horicon Marsh, so there are many animal and bird lovers passing through.

The Marsh is about 32,000 acres of very important wetland, which provides habitat for many animals, including several endangered species. It's also an extremely important rest stop and flyaway for migrating Canada geese and ducks. The Marsh is about five miles from here, and people come from all over the world to hike, bike, fish, hunt, kayak, and generally immerse themselves in wildlife. There are many muskrats, beaver and deer, and we have the third largest freshwater cattail marsh in the United States. Almost three hundred different species of birds have been identified, so it's a birder's paradise.

Unfortunately for the geese and ducks, there has been a lot of experimenting with what birds are wanted here. Some years they want a lot of geese, and the next year they decide they're a nuisance, so they want ducks instead. The birds are getting confused. Farmers used to plant corn, which geese like, so they'd come when the corn was being harvested, but then the farmers complained there were too many geese. Now they scare the geese away. There's also the fact that golf courses and people along the river don't like to encourage them to nest, so they use gun noise that fires off automatically to scare them away. We used to have such huge flocks. All of a sudden you'd see an enormous cloud of geese rising in unison. Very dramatic and moving.

The Horicon Marsh is recognized as a Wetland of International Importance, as a Globally Important Bird Area, and is also part of the Ice Age Scientific Reserve. It's very good for business and the local economy. Probably twenty years from now there will be many more business attractions, and the marsh will continue to draw people. I also think the area will continue to grow as people come to study the extensive Native American relics still to be found here.

∞

I always thought it would be great to own a home that had been in my family for twenty generations with everything in the attic having belonged to some relative at some time or other. I'd have all these tangible objects that I could touch and hold—*oh, this doll's tea set belonged to my great great grandmother when she was a little girl,* or *that's my grandfather's Civil War sword*—and I'd feel as if I could actually touch the past. It's that sense of continuity, that one thing follows from another.

One of the things I love about Mayville is there's such an active interest in history here. People are doing a lot to preserve the past, which to me makes it special. I'm involved in several projects, either historical or for beautification, that are dear to my heart and that I feel contribute to life in Mayville.

When I first returned, having improved the appearance of the interstate bridge in Narrowsburg, I figured why not improve the bridge down on Main Street? I wanted to get flower boxes to add to its beauty. There were no lights on either side of the bridge, so at night it was dark and felt unsafe. When the town was making plans to redo Main Street, our Main Street Mayville volunteer organization suggested putting lights on the bridge to make it safer. Fortunately, the mayor liked the plans, and it definitely improved that stretch for people walking or driving back and forth at night.

Another project we're working on is trying to get a mural in the Post Office cleaned so people can enjoy looking at it. It was painted in 1932 as a WPA project by Peter Rotier, whose style was very similar to the famous Mexican artist, Diego Rivera. "Wisconsin Rural Scene" is a wonderful farm landscape and now has historic significance. Many people aren't aware of the mural because it badly needs cleaning and some good lighting to show it off.

White Limestone School
Photo by George Frederick

I'm a board member of the Mayville Historical Society and we are working on several projects. One is the restoration of the cupola of the White Limestone School that almost dates back to Wisconsin's admission to the Union. By 1857, Mayville's small frame schoolhouse could no longer support its growing population, so the town built a sixty by forty foot structure out of white limestone quarried nearby. The population continued to grow over the next twenty years, mostly due to the iron smelting industry, and it was necessary to double the size of the existing building. Friedrich Fischer, a local mason, was the master builder of the 1876 addition, including a pillared portico and cupola, which gave the school quite a dignified appearance. The original school bell called the children to class twice a day and rang at recess for many years. I'll never forget that sound—the bell ringing, followed by happy shrieks as we poured out of the school for recess. I'm one of the few remaining people who went to every grade at the White Limestone School.

In the late 1960s, the deteriorated cupola was removed, and the schoolhouse stood without it for thirty years until a replica of the original was put back. A spotlight shines on the cupola at night and makes the town look so beautiful. The schoolhouse really is a magnificent building and has been listed on the National Registry of Historic Places since 1976. The original bell from 1857 is now on display inside the building.

Another passion of mine is trying to save trees. My mother was in love with her trees, especially elms. We'd be driving with her, and I can remember her saying, "Isn't that a beautiful tree?" That love of old trees seems to have dropped down to me, so I'm still trying to save them whenever I can.

☙

Daisy was a little put out when Chip came to live at River's Bend Inn, but they worked out a manageable relationship. Chip came to me when James and Susie moved back to the US from Singapore where they had him since he was a puppy. They flew him to Milwaukee where I picked him up. Since they weren't settled anywhere they could keep him, I took him. He has some unresolved issues, probably having to do with being separated from his family, and acts out in a way that's less than ideal for running a B & B, but I care about him and am willing to deal with him.

I had Daisy for twelve-and-a-half years, and I can pretty much say we were joined at the hip. She was my best pal, very sensitive, intelligent, and totally attuned to me. Whenever my daughter Olivia called, she wanted to talk to Daisy, whom she adored. Daisy knew exactly when I was getting ready to hang up and wanted to have one last bark into the telephone. Daisy died unexpectedly just as I was finishing this book. My life seemed to stop. I felt as if a part of my soul departed way too early and my heart actually hurts with

Daisy admiring the view. North Carolina, 2004.

sadness. Anyone who has experienced the strong, almost magical bond with an animal knows what I'm talking about. Daisy's absence is just so...ever present. I've had an outpouring of understanding and sympathy from friends and family who know what Daisy meant to me and loved her also, but it feels as if the grief will never end. Maybe it never does.

My love of animals certainly wasn't passed down from my parents, since neither was a great animal lover, but I always was. That photo Grandpa took of me when I was about five where I'm sitting on the floor in his studio, big bow in my perfectly curled ringlets, carrying on an intense conversation with group of stuffed animals spread around me, says it all. In those days, I believed animals had human emotions, and I don't think I've changed my mind over all these years.

I could never work in an animal shelter. I'd be bringing them all home. In the weekly paper there's usually a report from the animal shelter with the 'dog of the week' or the 'cat of the week,' and I always read it. Once I was tempted to adopt a dog with three legs. Until a few days ago I kept a clipping about a three-legged kitten named Carter.

I guess I'm drawn to creatures who have a handicap and need an extra boost. I asked for the runt of the litter when I got Daisy. Chip's a handful. In Narrowsburg, I had a duck who was rejected by her community, perhaps because she was the ugliest duck I've ever seen. She used to walk right into the kitchen and come sit on my lap. When I think back on my life, I imagine it might have something to do with my having been so physically delicate and incapacitated as a child. I also think of the men in my life and how each one had an infirmity. Eric had been nearly paralyzed in a car accident and left with damage; Harold had had polio when he was a child and walked with a limp; Jack had terrible chronic pain in his back, and Jim had the severe neurological problem in his foot. Even David had to carry around that huge chip on his shoulder. Maybe I'm just a soft touch, or maybe I can see how infirmities can be overcome with enough determination and love.

FULL CIRCLE

Painting of Daisy and me by Dan Daly. 2007

❦ 27 ❧

In Love with Iambic Pentameter

B ecause I spent so much of my childhood in bed reading, I fell in love with words. I had a great vocabulary early on and appreciated the nuances in the meaning of words. To this day, I love the rhythm of words. When my mother went to school, children had to memorize poetry and I remember being impressed by how much she could recite, especially Henry Wadsworth Longfellow. The rhythm and imagery of "Paul Revere's Ride" and "Hiawatha" have never left me. In my English classes in poetry, I was always good at identifying the rhythms and rhymes. Today, schools don't seem to require children to memorize. Our language, which is an incredibly beautiful one, is becoming less impressive and less interpretive as words get abbreviated and even eliminated to save time on the computer. I think the decline in language destroys people's ability to interpret finer things.

I never seem to have enough time to read as much as I want; I would like to be able to finish the newspaper every

245

day, but can't. I have a problem when I get a book from the library that I get involved with because all I want to do is read it, and then I don't do anything else. I tend to discipline myself and just read at night. I primarily read non-fiction and especially like biographies, autobiographies, and diaries.

I still have my college English books with my whole collection of poetry that I love. One of my favorite poems is "Thanatopsis" by William Cullen Bryant. The title means "an expression of somebody's thoughts about death."

"Renaissance" by Edna St. Vincent Millay, written when she was only twenty, is one of my favorites. It's got a lovely lyrical tone and her words create amazing imagery and sort of a mystical feeling. Although it's intensely personal—talking about her inner spiritual quest—it's got a very universal quality that the reader can relate to. That's why it's so powerful.

All I could see from where I stood
Were three long mountains and a wood;
I turned and looked the other way,
And saw three islands in a bay.

I love the rhythm—

So with my eyes I traced the line
Of the horizon, thin and fine,
Straight around till I was come
Back from where I started from;
And all I saw from where I stood
Was three long mountains and a wood.
Over these things I could not see;
These were the things that bounded me;
And I could touch them with my hand,
Almost, I thought, from where I stand.

It's a very long poem and goes on with the narrator buried underground.

Long had I lain thus, craving death,
When quietly the earth beneath
Gave way, and inch by inch, so great
At last had grown the crushing weight,
Into the earth I sank till I
Full six feet under ground did lie,
And sank no more, —there is no weight
Can follow here, however great.

Then the last part is:

The world stands out on either side
No wider than the heart is wide;
Above the world is stretched the sky,
No higher than the soul is high.
The heart can push the sea and land
Farther away on either hand;
The soul can split the sky in two
And let the face of God shine through.
But East and West will pinch the heart
That can not keep them pushed apart;
And he whose soul is flat—the sky
Will cave in on him by and by.

Isn't that great?

One of my other favorite poems is Robert Frost's "Stopping By Woods on a Snowy Evening."

Animal Farm and *1984* by George Orwell are two very important books, which I think everyone should read today. Orwell was really way ahead of his time in his analogy of how pigs run everything, and the other farm animals in the barnyard just have to follow along!

There's a short little book called *The Law* by Frederick Bastiat, written in 1848 which I'd like all my grandchildren to read. I read it in the 1960s and it had a great influence on me.

My grandfather once gave me this anonymous poem about not quitting when things go wrong:

When things go wrong, as they sometimes will,
When the road you're trudging seems all up hill,
When the funds are low and the debts are high,
And you want to smile, but you have to sigh,
When care is pressing you down a bit,
Rest! if you must; but don't you quit.

Life is queer with its twists and turns,
As every one of us sometimes learns,
And many a failure turns about
When he might have won had he stuck it out;
Don't give up, though the pace seems slow;
You might succeed with another blow.

Often the goal is nearer than
It seems to a faint and faltering man,
Often the struggler has given up
When he might have captured the victor's cup.
And he learned too late, when the night slipped down,
How close he was to the golden crown.

Success is failure turned inside out;
The silver tint of the clouds of doubt;
And you never can tell how close you are,
It may be near when it seems afar;
So stick to the fight when you're hardest hit;
It's when things seem worst that you mustn't quit.

I'm not sure what this quote is from, but I love its rhythm and what it's saying:

Far far away and way way afar, it's over the moon and the
sea; wherever you're going that's wherever you are and no-
body knows it but me.

Another person whose writing I enjoyed was Cornelia Otis Skinner. She was an actress and humor writer. I heard a lecture by her once at the University of Wisconsin and thought she was terrific. She lived in Smithtown, Long Island where Jim's sister lived (and where I was married) and we went to her home for lunch once when we were visiting Alma and Ham. Coincidentally, her husband was Alden Blodgett, who was "a kissing cousin" of mine.

Skinner did wonderful one-woman performances of character sketches she wrote, and also wrote short humorous pieces for upscale publications like *The New Yorker*. She co-authored *Our Hearts Were Young and Gay*, which was on the Best Seller list for many weeks and was eventually made into a movie. It was a hilarious description of the two authors' European tour in the 1920s, just after they graduated from college. I'm sure I enjoyed it because it reminded me of some of Gloria's and my escapades!

I like this one too:

Reflections on Risk.
To laugh is to risk appearing the fool, to weep is to risk appearing sentimental, to reach out for another is to risk involvement, to expose feelings is to risk exposing your true self, to place your ideas, your dreams before the crowd is to risk their loss, to love is to risk not being loved in return, to live is to risk dying, to hope is to risk despair, to try is to risk failure, but risks must be taken because the greatest hazard is to risk nothing. The person who risks nothing does nothing, has nothing and is nothing. He may avoid suffering and sorrow but he cannot learn, feel, change, grow, live, love. Chained by his certitude he is a slave... he has forfeited freedom. Only a person who risks is free.
[Author unknown]

I have a clipping on my bulletin board that talks about the writer having a friend who he keeps meaning to see but never gets around to. He's always saying to himself, "Tomorrow, I say. Tomorrow I will call on him just to show that I'm thinking of him." But tomorrow comes and goes; finally he gets a telegram that his friend died. The last part says:

Remember to always say what you mean. If you love someone, tell them. Don't be afraid to express yourself. Reach out and tell someone what they mean to you. Because when you decide that it is the right time it might be too late. Seize the day. Never have regrets. And most importantly, stay close to your friends and family, for they have helped make you the person that you are today.

Reading this, of course, reminds me of how I lost touch with Gloria. I'm determined not to let that happen with anybody else I know, whether family or friend.

IN LOVE WITH IAMBIC PENTAMETER

"And most importantly, stay close to your friends and
family, for they have helped make you the person
that you are today."
Standing, l-r: Olivia, James, Susie
Seated, l-r: Sarah, me and Daisy, Emily, Abby.

❦ *Last... (for Now)* ❧ *Conversation with My Granddaughter*

R ecently Sarah visited me for a week. On a balmy summer evening, we were having dinner out on the terrace and she thought it would be fun to give me the Proust Questionnaire. Apparently, Marcel Proust was asked these questions by a friend—once at the age of thirteen and again at around twenty. So, with the sound of cicadas and the fountain in the background, the smell of corn on the cob roasting over the grill, Daisy and Chip lying at our feet, we went through the questionnaire. These are only some of the questions and answers.

Sarah: Nonie, what do you fear most?

Me. Dying. But for me it's not, like for so many people, out of fear. It's because I really want to know what's going to happen next. When I hear something might happen twenty years from now—like a landing on Mars—I think...doubt I'll be around, but I'd really like to know if they get to Mars!

Sarah: Nonie, if they get to Mars and you're gone, I'll sent word via balloon. Promise!

Me: I just don't know how much faith I have that there's something on the other side. Sometimes I think mankind has such tremendous conceit of self-importance thinking, *how could there could be anything going on afterward?* I wish I could have the faith that some people I know have; they're sure there is something after death. I just have too many questions that have not been answered.

Sarah: What profession other than your own would you most like to have had?

Me: I'd like to have been an interior designer. I certainly did a fair amount of interior design with houses I bought and sold but I would have liked to do a lot more. I always loved to make something into something else—beautify, create an atmosphere. Or, I would have liked to be an artist and paint portraits. I didn't do it because I started painting walls instead, so didn't have time for art.

Sarah: What profession would you least have liked?

Me: That's easy—an undertaker. We knew several when I was growing up. When I was fifteen, the Mouls, one of the undertaker families in Mayville, had a guy working for them and I had puppy love for him. I probably thought being an undertaker's wife wouldn't be that bad....

Sarah: What trait do you like most in yourself?

Me. I'd say loyalty.

Sarah: What trait do you most dislike?

Me: That would be the fact that I'm afraid to do some things that I'd like to do.

Sarah: That's so interesting because if I look at anyone in my life, you emulate the person who did the most different and adventurous things. I would never think of fear as something you had and I think you passed that lack of fear down to my dad.

Me: That's interesting. Your mother once said to me, which I always considered a great compliment, "You know, if I had to go out west in the pioneer days with someone, it would be you. If something came up unexpectedly, you'd figure out how to handle it."

Sarah: Same with my dad. He always says if we don't know how to do something we'll figure it out. It's easy to do something with him because he'll just go ahead; he doesn't have to figure it all out way in advance. Let's go down that road, get off on a side road, he'll say. He has an adventurous spirit. I see that totally in you. What trait do you most value in others?

Me: Sense of humor.

Sarah: Most deplore?

Me: People who are devious, people you can't trust what they're saying.

Sarah: When and where were you the happiest?

Me: I think either when I was going with Charlie or when I was in my late teenage years living with my mother. She gave me a sense of security more than when I was out on my own. I used to think, *my mother is sixty years old. What if she dies? It's going to be so awful.* She was probably my real life hero. I admired and respected her so much. I didn't appreciate it much when growing up, but in retrospect I do. My mother used to say she wouldn't be intimidated to walk up and shake the president's hand, that everybody is born, dies the same way.

Sarah: You got that right! You did more than shake a president's hand!

Me: Very funny, Sarah!

Sarah: What would be your greatest extravagance?

Me: I'm not an extravagant person but I like extravagance. It would probably be to be able to take a trip any time I feel like it and stay in fabulous places on a whim.

Sarah: What was your favorite occupation?

Me: Being president of the United States.

Sarah: But, Nonie, you didn't do that!

Me: I would have liked to!

Sarah: What's been the hardest thing for you to do?

Me: It's been hardest for me to get up and speak. I admire that about you, Sarah, that you can do that so effortlessly.

Sarah: What's the most overrated virtue?

Me: Celibacy.

Sarah: That's wonderful! I love you, Nonie! My mother would laugh so hard. She'd agree.

Sarah: What's something you like about getting older?

Me: I've gotten more outspoken. I used to just think something about someone, but now I really try to say it if it's good. For example, if something looks good on a person I make a point of saying it instead of just thinking it. Recently I was talking to a person on the phone about my phone service. At the end of the call, I told her she'd been so nice and helpful. She said I'd made her day. It was a small thing, but small things can change a person's day. When you're older you can get away with sentiment like that.

Sarah: What's your greatest achievement?

Me: Keeping myself alive all this time.

Sarah: Nonie, I swear to God you sleep in Tupperware.

Me: What do you mean?

Sarah: Tupperware preserves the freshness. I hope I have those genes.

Me: The secret is to be active in doing something you're interested in. That's what keeps you young and going.

Sarah: If heaven exists what would you like God to say to you when you arrive at the Pearly Gates?

Me: Hmmmm. (Interminable pause....)

Sarah: I'd like Him to say, "Wasn't that amazing!"

Me: I can't think of a better answer than that.

Sarah: You can't steal my answer, Nonie.

Me: Then I'll have to think on that one and get back to you.

Sarah: What's your favorite sound?

Me: Crickets, the fountain probably. Just like we're hearing right now.

⌘

If Sarah had asked me my favorite time of day I'd have had an easy answer. I'd say evening. I love the sense of evening arriving when you can sit down and have nothing more you have to do that day. In winter when it gets dark early, I can light the fire, turn the soft lights on earlier and read to my heart's content.

When I used to go to Florida, I loved going down to the beach and enjoying a glass of wine while I sat and watched the sun go down. I noticed people coming out, lining up down at the end of the street to watch. It's odd, they stood there and watched the sun go down, but as soon as it slipped below the horizon, they left. They were really missing something. Sometimes the light afterwards is much more spectacular than it is before. There's a space, an interval where the waves die down and everything has that mysterious pink and dove-colored light—soft and beautiful.

I love to watch the sunset here, too. As the sun slips behind the trees on the far bank of the Rock River, it makes them cast shadows—like footbridges—reaching over to my side of the river. I watch the afterglow spread slowly as it reflects off the bend in the river.

Other Books by Safe Goods

The ADD and ADHD Diet Expanded	$ 10.95
ADD, The Natural Approach	$ 5.95
Testosterone is your Friend	$ 8.95
Eye Care Naturally	$ 8.95
The Natural Prostate Cure	$ 6.95
The Minerals You Need	$ 4.95
The Smart Brain Train	$ 7.95
New Hope for Serious Diseases	$ 7.95
What is Beta Glucan?	$ 4.95
Cancer Disarmed Expanded	$ 7.95
The Vertical System	$ 9.95
Overcoming Senior Moments Expanded	$ 9.95
Crissy the CowPot Gets Her Wish!	$ 9.95
Lower Cholesterol without Drugs	$ 6.95
The Secrets of Staying Young	$ 11.95
Worse Than Global Warming	$ 9.95
2012 Airborne Prophesy	$ 16.95
The Natural Diabetes Cure	$ 8.95
Rx for Computer Eyes	$ 8.95
Kids First: Health with No Interference	$ 16.95
Prevent Cancer, Strokes, Heart Attacks	$ 11.95
Flying Above the Glass Ceiling	$ 14.95

For a complete listing of books visit our web site: www.safegoodspub.com to order or call in the U.S.

for a free catalog (888) NATURE-1